The History of Country Music

TITLES IN THIS SERIES INCLUDE:

The History of Alternative Rock

The History of American Pop

The History of Jazz

The History of Music Videos

The History of Rap and Hip-Hop

The History of Rock and Roll

THE MUSIC LIBRARY

The History of Country Music

Stuart A. Kallen

LUCENT BOOKS
A part of Gale, Cengage Learning

GALE
CENGAGE Learning™

Detroit • New York • San Francisco • New Haven, Conn • Waterville, Maine • London

©2012 Gale, Cengage Learning

LIBRARY OF CONGRESS CATALOGING-IN-PUBLICATION DATA

Kallen, Stuart A., 1955-
    The history of country music / by Stuart A. Kallen.
        pages cm -- (The music library)
    Includes bibliographical references and index.
    ISBN 978-1-4205-0737-9 (hardcover)
    1. Country music--History and criticism--Juvenile literature. I. Title.
    ML3524.K36 2012
    781.64209--dc23   2012002275

Lucent Books
27500 Drake Rd
Farmington Hills MI 48331

ISBN-13: 978-1-4205-0737-9
ISBN-10: 1-4205-0737-0

Printed in the United States of America
1 2 3 4 5 6 7 16 15 14 13 12

CONTENTS

FOREWORD

I n the nineteenth century, English novelist Charles Kingsley wrote, "Music speaks straight to our hearts and spirits, to the very core and root of our souls. . . . Music soothes us, stirs us up . . . melts us to tears." As Kingsley stated, music is much more than just a pleasant arrangement of sounds. It is the resonance of emotion, a joyful noise, a human endeavor that can soothe the spirit or excite the soul. Musicians can also imitate the expressive palette of the earth, from the violent fury of a hurricane to the gentle flow of a babbling brook.

The word *music* is derived from the fabled Greek muses, the children of Apollo who ruled the realms of inspiration and imagination. Composers have long called upon the muses for help and insight. Music is not merely the result of emotions and pleasurable sensations, however.

Music is a discipline subject to formal study and analysis. It involves the juxtaposition of creative elements such as rhythm, melody, and harmony with intellectual aspects of composition, theory, and instrumentation. Like painters mixing red, blue, and yellow into thousands of colors, musicians blend these various elements to create classical symphonies, jazz improvisations, country ballads, and rock-and-roll tunes.

Throughout centuries of musical history, individual musical elements have been blended and modified in infinite ways. The resulting sounds may convey a whole range of moods, emotions, reactions, and messages. Music, then, is both an expression and reflection of human experience and emotion.

The foundations of modern musical styles were laid down by the first ancient musicians who used wood, rocks, animal skins—and their own bodies—to re-create the sounds of the natural world in which they lived. With their hands, their feet, and their very breath they ignited the passions of listeners and moved them to their feet. The dancing, in turn, had a mesmerizing and hypnotic effect that allowed people to transcend their worldly concerns. Through music they could achieve a level of shared experience that could not be found in other forms of communication. For this reason, music has always been part of religious endeavors, from ancient Egyptian spiritual ceremonies to modern Christian masses. And it has inspired dance movements from kings and queens spinning the minuet to punk rockers slamming together in a mosh pit.

By examining musical genres ranging from Western classical music to rock and roll, readers will find a new understanding of old music and develop an appreciation for new sounds. Books in Lucent's Music Library focus on the music, the musicians, the instruments, and on music's place in cultural history. The songs and artists examined may be easily found in the CD and sheet music collections of local libraries so that readers may study and enjoy the music covered in the books. Informative sidebars, annotated bibliographies, and complete indexes highlight the text in each volume and provide young readers with many opportunities for further discussion and research.

American Music

The term *country music* is used today to describe songs played on country radio stations and in videos shown on country music television channels. The videos feature handsome men and pretty women dressed in tight jeans, cowboy boots, and other western gear. They dance and sing about love, despair, partying, and the good ol' U.S.A. The music rings out on stringed instruments—guitars, mandolins, banjos, fiddles, and pedal steel guitars.

The sounds of modern country music artists such as Kenny Chesney, Toby Keith, and Carrie Underwood are aimed at a twenty-first-century audience. The music often merges big rock beats, slick lyrics, and seamless digital production. Country singer Jason Aldean even raps to a hip-hop beat about cornbread, biscuits, and his homeys gathered around a campfire.

While the top artists in the digital age sell millions of compact discs (CDs), music downloads, and cell phone ringtones, the sounds of contemporary country can be traced back several generations to the 1930s, '40s, and '50s. Today's country music is built on a foundation of sweet gospel-tinged harmonies pioneered by the Carter Family and the hot mandolin picking of bluegrass founder Bill Monroe. Modern artists also find inspiration in the western swing fiddle arrangements of Bob Wills and the sad, lonesome love songs of Hank Williams.

The Music of Appalachia

Country music was born in the southern Appalachian Mountains, the green rolling hills that dominate the American countryside in parts of the Carolinas, Virginia, West Virginia, Kentucky, and Tennessee. The area was first settled in the mid-1700s by English and Scots-Irish immigrants who brought with them fiddles, guitars, mandolins, and other easy-to-carry instruments. The rocky, hilly terrain was inaccessible to all but the most determined travelers, and the descendents of the first settlers remained extremely isolated. With little in the way of outside entertainment, almost everybody sang and played an instrument. Music based on ancient English and Irish songs was popular, and vocal church music, sung in groups with no instrumental accompaniment, was also a very important part of life.

At the beginning of the twentieth century, the modern world rapidly encroached on the Appalachian people. Railroads, coal mines, textile mills, iron and steel mills, and oil fields were built across the rural South. Men and women who formerly spent their days hunting, fishing, and farming started digging in mines, punching factory clocks, and laboring on trains and drilling rigs. These changes brought new influences into traditional music. People began to sing about their common problems, such as longing for the old homestead, suffering from a broken heart, and working for low wages.

A Healing Tonic

The introduction of radio and record players also brought about changes to country songs. The music of African American blues and gospel, Louisiana Cajun, western cowboy, and even jazz formed a rich cultural stew as the songs of Appalachia spread across southern and western America. Although the style was derided in big cities as

Country music stars Lady Antebellum— Charles Kelley, Hillary Scott, and Dave Haywood— were among the top selling artists in all music categories in 2010.

hillbilly music, it was, in fact, true American roots music, influenced by millions of hardworking, patriotic folks.

Traditional country music is divided into categories, such as bluegrass, western swing, honky-tonk, and the Nashville sound. Over the decades, however, this music has been blended with pop, rock, blues, and other modern sounds. This led to the creation of new genres such as country pop, Americana, neotraditionalism, and alternative or alt-country.

Along with the song styles, the country music business itself has grown and changed with the times. The exploding popularity of Country Music Television (CMT) in the mid-1980s introduced country-oriented videos, concerts, movies, and programs to a new record-buying audience. In the early 1990s, the Internet provided a way for independent country music radio stations to broadcast throughout the world. Within a few years, dozens of stations were formatting their playlists to cater to fans of specific country styles, including bluegrass, up-tempo dance, classics, contemporary, outlaw, and more. In the 2000s, the explosive growth of music downloads and online music stores made tens of thousands of country albums available to anyone with an Internet connection. Old catalogs of classic country acts dating back to the 1920s were digitized and downloaded by the millions.

Today country music remains big business. In 2010, even as the overall music industry suffered from a sales slump, nearly 44 million country music albums were sold. That figure represented nearly 30 percent of all albums sold that year, including those by alternative, rap, rock, and Latin performers. Country music stars like Taylor Swift, Lady Antebellum, and the Zac Brown Band were among the top-selling artists in every category.

While some country artists have grown rich, the aim of country music has changed little since its early incarnation in the Appalachian Mountains. Country music is and was a healing tonic for anyone with a broken heart, the lonesome blues, or just a basic urge to dance the night away.

CHAPTER 1

Country Roots

Country music is, first and foremost, American music, and its story begins with the founding of the country itself. From the moment the first English settlers came to the New World, they were singing and playing folk songs that dated to sixteenth-century England, Ireland, and Scotland. Most people during this era were illiterate. The events of the day were not written down in books, but rather immortalized in songs that were passed down from generation to generation. The songs were about suffering, love, death, and dishonor. The words described the world in personal terms that all listeners could easily understand.

The lyrics of the old English songs changed over the centuries in order to fit in with American experiences and culture. Country music journalist Steven D. Price describes how songs evolved:

Names of characters and locales were Americanized: "The Oxford Girl" became "The Knoxville Girl," while "Bonnie George Campbell" turned into "Georgie Collins." Titles of nobility bit the dust: "Lord Randal" found himself in some parts of America as "Jimmy Randal," "Sir Lionel" became "Old Bangum."[1]

The old songs were affected by the American temperament as well. Long British ballads, or songs that told a story, were drastically shortened by pioneers. The thirty-five-verse

"The Lass of Loch Royal," for instance, transformed into the three-verse "Who's Gonna Shoe Your Pretty Little Foot?"

Americans often added overwrought emotion and sentimentality to British songs. The renowned country music scholar Bill C. Malone, who heard traditional ballads while growing up in rural East Texas in the 1930s, describes the songs:

[They were] lonesome old sentimental tunes sung by my mother about maidens who died of unrequited [unreturned] love . . . little orphans whose deaths on the bitterly cold street were but a prelude to a joyous [reunion] with Mother in Heaven, and eastbound trains that carried penniless little children to reunions with their poor blind fathers in prison.[2]

The expressive emotional feeling was coupled with the American interpretation of morality. While British folk songs often had graphic—and humorous—descriptions of sexual relations, Americans quickly dropped these lyrics. Americans, however, were quite tolerant of violence, especially between lovers. As Price writes: "Victims were shot, stabbed, drowned, poisoned, or otherwise done in."[3] American morals demanded that songs attach stern warnings to bloody tales. For example, the last verse of "Pearl Bryan," a song about two men murdering a girl and cutting off her head, advises young ladies to stay at home and never trust strange men.

Religious Roots

The warnings attached to love ballads were called for at a time when religion played a central role in the lives of country people. Sedate British hymns, some dating back to the tenth century, were deemed inadequate for the exuberant religious revivals that periodically swept across the United States in the nineteenth century. As hundreds of people gathered in backwoods churches, they turned to songbooks such as *The Southern Harmony*, published in 1835, which contained more than three hundred Americanized religious songs.

Again, folk melodies served as a basis for new words more appropriate for the American experience. Songbooks

Evangelists Ira David Sankey and Dwight Lyman Moody (right to left) published songbooks that were extremely popular in the late nineteenth and early twentieth centuries.

published by singer Ira Sankey and evangelist Dwight L. Moody in the late nineteenth century were extremely popular, selling more than 50 million copies between 1875 and 1908. The Sankey-Moody books contained songs such as "When the Roll is Called Up Yonder," "The Drunkard's Lone Child," and "Life's Railway to Heaven" that had a decidedly American take on salvation.

Religious songs were often performed by church quartets, and many of the first nationally popular country music stars, such as Asher Sizemore and Little Jimmie, started their musical careers singing in gospel choirs. Their four-part church harmony singing style became central to country music in later years.

Whiskey, Food, and Music

Songbook publishers hired talented quartets to travel throughout the South, singing their songs—and selling their songbooks—on Sundays in churches. During the rest of the week, groups of traveling entertainers called minstrels played in taverns, theaters, traveling medicine shows, and on steamboats and trains.

Musicians played guitars, banjos, mandolins, and other instruments. But violins (or fiddles), which were small, loud, and cheap to repair, were especially popular. Nearly every social gathering in the South required a fiddler to entertain the crowd. Fiddlers played when neighbors gathered to raise a barn, harvest a crop, or celebrate a milestone. Fiddlers were called upon to play dozens of tunes, often based on Irish jigs and English reels, sometimes playing solo, sometimes in groups. As top-selling country fiddler Clinton Gregory recalls, many of the fiddlers were taught to play by their relatives:

> I learned to play the fiddle from my father . . . who was a champion fiddler back in Virginia. His dad was a fiddler, and *his* dad. It goes back five generations. Playing square dances when I was a kid is basically how I learned to play. The three main ingredients for a professional square dance [are] plenty of bootleg whiskey to drink, plenty of food, and good music.[4]

While the fiddler and his bow ruled the Southern barn dance, by the end of the nineteenth century there were plenty of guitar players around. Rural guitar players were often influenced by African American musicians who played blues, ragtime, and gospel songs. Black musicians also played banjos, instruments with roots in ancient Africa. By the late nineteenth century, rural whites had adapted the banjo to their musical styles, and it became one of the basic instruments of twentieth-century country music.

Hillbilly Music

While stringed instruments were "old as the hills," in 1877 a mechanical invention took country music beyond its rural roots to millions of eager listeners. When Thomas Edison invented the phonograph, he believed it might be useful for dictation in a business setting. No one thought of selling music for the machine, which later became known as a record player, until 1891, when Columbia Records printed a catalog to sell wax cylinders containing such hits as "The Esquimaux [Eskimo] Dance," a clarinet solo backed by barking dogs and a hammer striking an anvil.

People were eager to hear these primitive offerings, however, and the record business quickly kicked into high gear. By 1895 Columbia was selling hundreds of cylinders a day. In 1900 the company offered more than five thousand selections. By that time, the flat record had been perfected, and 10-inch (25.4cm) discs sold for as little as a dollar.

In the early 1900s dozens of record labels released songs that would come to be categorized as country music. Singers such as Cal Stewart, Billy Murray, and Billy Golden released humorous songs about characters referred to as country bumpkins, or hillbillies.

While some performers considered the hillbilly label a useful marketing term that helped sell records, others rejected the expression. It was seen as an insult that spread harmful stereotypes about Southerners. These negative images were on display in a 1900 report in the *New York Journal* that described people at a Southern square dance: "A Hill-Billie is a free and untrammeled white citizen of Alabama, who lives in the hills, has no [job] to speak of, dresses as he can, talks as he pleases, drinks whiskey when he can get it, and fires off his revolver as the fancy takes him."[5]

Topping the Charts

In 1922, two country musicians who happened to be in New York City walked into the offices of Victor Records unannounced and declared that they were ready to record some music. Fiddlers Eck Robertson and Henry Gilliland were dressed as cowboys, and the men impressed Victor executives with their music. Within weeks the company released the first record with the word *hillbilly* on the label—the lightning-fast fiddle tune "Sallie Gooden" backed by "Arkansas Traveler."

Although they had to compete with other new forms of recorded music, such as jazz and blues, hillbilly records charted respectable sales numbers. In 1922 "Wreck of the Southern Old 97," written by former mill hand Henry Whitter about a 1903 train accident, sold 1 million copies. That same year the hillbilly tune "It Ain't Gonna Rain No Mo,'" by Wendell Hall, sold a phenomenal 2 million copies. Hillbilly music was topping the charts, and in 1922 alone it helped push record sales figures over $105 million.

With the astonishing success of hillbilly music, New York record producers began combing the South for talent. In the summer of 1927 Victor Records sent talent scout Ralph Peer to Bristol, Virginia—in the heart of Appalachia—where he managed to audition a dizzying variety of gospel singers, string bands, balladeers, and others in a twelve-day marathon. Two of the acts signed, Jimmie Rodgers and the Carter Family, quickly became legends of country music.

The Carter Family, from the appropriately named Poor Valley, Virginia, consisted of Alvin P. Carter (known as A.P.), his wife, Sara, and his sister-in-law Maybelle. The innovative trio based its sound on sweet singing arrangements with soaring three-part harmonies. This new sound shifted the focus of country music to vocals, an area that had achieved scant attention by earlier hillbilly singers. A.P. was a musicologist—someone who studies music—and he "unearthed" or wrote most of the group's material, along with Maybelle and Sara. These songs, including "Wildwood Flower," "I'm Thinking Tonight of My Blue Eyes," "Will the Circle Be Unbroken," and "Hello Stranger," sold millions of records. Today the Carter Family songs are country standards that have been covered by almost everybody in the business.

Sara Carter was the first female country music star, and Maybelle's thumb picking, later known as Carter picking, made the guitar a lead instrument for the first time on record. Although the group disbanded in the early 1940s, their

Country music pioneer A.P. Carter sings with his wife Sara and sister-in-law Maybelle (left to right) at their home in Poor Valley, Virginia, in 1941. The Carter Family songs have become widely covered country music standards.

music influenced a generation of country and rock musicians in the decades that followed. When Maybelle died in 1978, folksinger Ed Badeaux wrote that the Carters' greatest contribution to country music was "the way in which they perpetuated the traditional Anglo-Saxon [English] ballad, making it live anew in the hearts of succeeding generations of Americans."[6]

Turn Your Radio On

While the phonograph helped spur sales of hillbilly records, the popularity of country music was driven by another new form of mass communication. The first commercial radio station went on the air in 1920, and by the end of 1923 there were more than 550 broadcasting stations in the United States. Since no national programming existed, stations scrambled to fill hours of airtime with local entertainment.

Jimmie Rodgers—The Singing Brakeman

Jimmie Rodgers is one of the most popular country singers in history. Born in the tiny town of Meridian, Mississippi, in 1897, Rodgers learned to play music listening to black bluesmen and local Choctaw and Natchez Native American singers. In 1927 Rodgers traveled to New York City, where he recorded several songs for Victor Records and quickly became a best-selling artist. His song "Blue Yodel," also known as "T for Texas," sold five hundred thousand copies in mere months.

As a young man, Rodgers had worked as a brakeman on railroad trains. This earned him the nickname the Singing Brakeman, and he was often photographed holding his guitar, dressed in a railroad cap and denim jacket. Before his career was cut short by tuberculosis in 1933, Rodgers wrote dozens of hit songs that are now country standards, including "Waiting for a Train," "Travelin' Blues," and "Train Whistle Blues." The inscription on Rodgers' gravestone in Meridian sums up his sound: "His is the music of America. He sang the songs of the people he loved, of a young nation growing strong. His was an America of glistening rails, thundering boxcars, and rain-swept nights, of lonesome pines, great mountains, and a high blue sky."

Quoted in James L. Dickerson. *Mojo Triangle*. New York: Schirmer Trade Books, 2005, pp. 56–57.

In the South, scouts searched taverns and theaters for country music performers. One of the most popular country singers of the era, Eddy Arnold, was hired by agents while he was playing music on his front porch.

By 1924 listeners across the country could tune in on Saturday nights to the powerful 50,000-watt AM radio station WLS in Chicago, Illinois, to hear the *National Barn Dance.* This wildly popular radio show featured romantic country crooners, foot-tapping string bands, yodeling cowboys, cornball comics, and even barbershop quartets singing slick four-part harmonies. In 1932 the show was picked up by NBC and broadcast on thirty stations from coast to coast.

National Barn Dance made stars out of performers Bradley Kinkaid, Grandpa Jones, and cowgirl singer Pasty Montana—the first female country solo artist to sell a million records. The show also inspired a new group of country musicians. As country superstar Charley Pride says, "The radio was my only way of finding out what was out there beyond the cotton fields of home."[7]

Grand Ole Opry Every Saturday Night

The success of *National Barn Dance* inspired the creation of dozens of similar shows throughout the country, and none was more popular—or enduring—than the *Grand Ole Opry* on WSM in Nashville, Tennessee. When the show went on the air on December 26, 1925, people were able to hear it across a wide region because of WSM's powerful signal. The show, however, did not receive its name until 1927. After a formal program of classical opera music, *Opry* announcer George D. Hay came on the air and said, "For the past hour we have been listening to music taken largely from the Grand Opera, but from now on we will present the *Grand Ole Opry*."[8]

By the late 1930s the star of the *Opry* was the fiddler and singer Roy Acuff, "The King of Country Music." Acuff's band, the Smokey Mountain Boys, was the first to feature a Dobro, the name given to a slide guitar made by Gibson with what appears to be a metal hubcap attached to the face of the instrument. This metal resonator makes the Dobro, or resonator guitar, louder than an average guitar. The ringing Dobro was able to compete with Acuff's hard-charging singing style. "I rared back like I was going after the cows, the same way when I used to drive the cows out to pasture on the farm. In them hills up there . . . I sang loud,"[9] said Acuff. His hits, such as "The Great Speckled Bird," "Wabash Cannonball," "Wreck on the Highway," and "I Saw the Light," became instant country standards.

Bill Monroe's High, Lonesome Sound

In 1938 a mandolin player from Kentucky named Bill Monroe auditioned for the *Grand Ole Opry*. He played Jimmie Rodgers' "Mule Skinner Blues," backed by his band, the Bluegrass Boys. George D. Hay and Harry Stone, the *Opry*'s producers, were astounded by Monroe's lightning-fast licks. They hired him on the spot. As Monroe tells it, the producers said, "I had more perfect music for the station than any music they'd ever heard."[10] Radio listeners agreed, and Bill Monroe & His Bluegrass Boys were soon the most popular players on the show.

Today Monroe is considered the founding father of blue-grass music. The style depends on super-quick cascades of

Bill Monroe, the founding father of bluegrass music, performs on WSM radio in Nashville in 1940.

notes that are not written down on sheet music but rather improvised, or made up by the player on the spot. A standard bluegrass band like Monroe's consisted of five pieces: violin, mandolin, guitar, banjo, and stand-up bass. Other bluegrass bands occasionally add harmonica, piano, or Dobro to the mix.

Monroe's group also pioneered four-part bluegrass vocal harmony. *Opry* host George D. Hay described Monroe's unique voice: "There is that authentic wail in his high-pitched voice that one hears in the evening in the country when Mother Nature sighs and retires for the night."[11] Monroe himself described his band's harmony as that "high, lonesome sound."[12]

Bill Monroe's life story was similar to many who rose to stardom on the *Grand Ole Opry*. His family, from rural Rosine, Kentucky, was very poor but musically talented. Monroe's mother was an old-time fiddle player, and her brother Pendleton—later immortalized by Bill in the song "Uncle Pen"—also played the fiddle. Monroe's father had a high-pitched tenor voice, and his brother sang a harmony even higher than that. In addition to his family jam sessions, Monroe was inspired by an African American musician, Arnold Schultz, who often played guitar and fiddle at country dances in Rosine.

"Play It Good and Clean"

Playing on the *Grand Ole Opry* in the early 1940s helped make Bill Monroe & His Bluegrass Boys national stars. The restless Monroe, however, was not satisfied with the sound. As Monroe recalled in 1993, "I wanted a music of my own [and] I was going to play it the way I thought it should be played."[13] To that end, in 1945 Monroe put together an all-star band that would become synonymous with the term *bluegrass*. After hiring guitarist Lester Flatt, banjo picker Earl Scruggs, fiddler Chubby Wise, and bassist Howard "Cedric Rainwater" Watts, his new Bluegrass Boys burned up the stage at the Opry during the live shows.

In the years before it was routine for rock stars to receive hysterical adulation from fans, the Bluegrass Boys were a country music phenomenon. The audience screamed and yelled when they played their bluegrass "breakdowns" (songs played in double time). On tour the band broke attendance records wherever they went. Young musicians played the band's records at slower speeds on their phonographs, desperately trying to imitate the red-hot picking licks of Monroe and the other members of his band. The musical style became so popular that by 1953 folklorist Mike Seeger estimated that every Southern town with a population over a thousand had at least one amateur bluegrass band.

Today Monroe's songs—including "Blue Moon of Kentucky," "Uncle Pen," "In the Pines," "Molly & Tenbrooks," and "My Sweet Blue-Eyed Darlin'"—are bluegrass standards beloved by both musicians and fans. As to the secret of his success, Monroe stated plainly: "You always play it the best way you can. . . . Play it good and clean and play good melodies with it, but keep perfect time. It takes really good timing with bluegrass music, and it takes some good high voices to really deliver it right."[14]

"The Father of Bluegrass Music," as Monroe came to be known, died in 1996, just a few days short of his eighty-fifth birthday. By the time of his death, Monroe had seen his unique music style adapted by countless players from Nashville to Europe, Japan, and beyond. The reach of Monroe's bluegrass style was also extended by some of the 175 gifted musicians who played with His Bluegrass Boys over the years.

"Foggy Mountain Breakdown"

The first of Monroe's players to move on and create their own sound were Lester Flatt, Earl Scruggs, and Howard Watts, who quit the Bluegrass Boys in 1948 to form the Foggy Mountain Boys. Scruggs was easily the most popular player in the group. During his few years with Monroe, he had become a star in his own right. As bluegrass musician and author Bob Artis writes:

> Audiences just couldn't believe that anyone could play the banjo like Earl Scruggs. It was so fast and smooth, and there were so many notes, but all the melody and

Guitarist Lester Flatt and the popular banjo virtuoso Earl Scruggs perform with their band The Foggy Mountain Boys in the 1950s.

everything else was right there in the shower of banjo music. The crowds would roar every time Earl stepped to the microphone.[15]

Much of the thrill was the sound of the greased-lightning, three-finger picking style that Scruggs had perfected since he started playing the banjo in North Carolina at the age of four. In 1949 Scruggs wrote "Foggy Mountain Breakdown," a song that became an instant classic as part of every banjo player's repertoire. In 1967 "Foggy Mountain Breakdown" was used as the theme song for the hit movie *Bonnie and Clyde*.

By the late 1950s the Foggy Mountain Boys were taking their brand of blistering bluegrass breakdowns beyond the traditional country circuit to college campuses, where a new generation was eager to hear their sound. In 1962 Scruggs wrote "The Ballad of Jed Clampett," the theme song for the TV comedy *The Beverly Hillbillies*. Scruggs appeared on the extremely popular show numerous times with Lester Flatt, which helped make Flatt and Scruggs household names.

Stars of the Folk Revival

The growing popularity of bluegrass music in the 1960s was fueled by a series of folk festivals where pickers could gather to celebrate the music. The first event booked as a bluegrass festival was held on July 4, 1961, in a park in Luray, Virginia. Until this time bluegrass acts had performed solo or with other country acts, but never together at one show. The bluegrass festival, however, featured Bill Monroe, the Stanley Brothers, Jim & Jesse, and the Country Gentlemen all on one bill. The event quickly sold two thousand tickets—a huge number at the time—and the new venue for bluegrass music became an annual event.

Parking Lot Pickers

Country music journalist Steven D. Price describes the "parking lot picking" at a typical bluegrass festival:

The audience begins to arrive on Friday afternoon, quickly lining the road with their cars, trucks, and campers. No sooner do people reach the grounds than they unpack their instruments, raring to locate others with whom to make music. This aspect goes to the very heart of festivals, and indeed of Bluegrass itself. "Parking lot picker" is the term for an amateur who not only listens to Bluegrass, but who plays it. . . .

When the bands' buses pull up, it's as though the circus has come to town. Fans cluster around favorites, expressing their admiration and requesting tunes, while the professionals greet friends and sign autographs. . . . Professionals have no reluctance about "sitting in" with parking lot pickers, without feeling a need to show off or outshine their colleagues of the moment. Amateurs find the company stimulating and find that they are spurred on to play in ways they never knew they could. This kind of spontaneity and camaraderie marks any festival. . . . Long hair or crew cuts, bare feet or polished shoes, wash-and-wear shirts or tie-dyed tank tops, urban accents or rural drawls—the highest common denominator is a passion for Bluegrass.

Steven D. Price. *Old as the Hills.* New York: Viking Press, 1975, p. 92.

In 1966 Monroe held his own festival in Bean Blossom, Indiana, a place he often played in his early years. The first events were magical, with only three or four thousand people in attendance. By the 1980s Bean Blossom had grown one of the largest celebrations of bluegrass music anywhere in the world. In 2011 more than forty thousand people from across the globe descended on the otherwise sleepy town to listen to the best the bluegrass world had to offer. By that time, more than three hundred bluegrass festivals were being held around the world. Nearly every state hosted a festival, and this homegrown American celebration of bluegrass music could also be found in Japan, England, and elsewhere.

The musical entertainment at Bean Blossom and other bluegrass festivals was not limited to professionals. From the very beginning, an army of amateur players—called parking lot pickers—brought their own instruments to the festival. Impromptu jam sessions took place in parking lots, campgrounds, and picnic areas.

Doc Watson

The distinguished guitar picker Arthel "Doc" Watson is another bluegrass picker who gained recognition at 1960s bluegrass festivals. Like with Bill Monroe and the mandolin and Earl Scruggs and the banjo, Doc Watson's name is synonymous with bluegrass guitar wizardry.

Watson was born in Deep Gap, North Carolina, in 1923 and was blind since infancy. Like many pickers, he came from a musical family, and by the time he was a teenager, he had taught himself to play. Watson played rockabilly and western swing until he was in his thirties. Because his band did not have a fiddle player, Watson learned to pick out the complicated old-time songs on his guitar. He played the fiddle tunes "flat pick" style, that is, with a single "plectrum" guitar pick as opposed to finger picks.

Doc Watson (seated) and his son Merle, both known for their guitar playing and seen here in 1960, toured together until Merle's death in 1985.

MerleFest

In 1988, three years after the tragic death of guitarist Merle Watson, his father, renowned guitar picker Arthel "Doc" Watson held a series of benefit concerts in Wilkesboro, North Carolina. The concerts were held to raise money for the local community. The first MerleFest used two flatbed trucks for stages. Since that time it has grown into one of the premier bluegrass and country music festivals in America. Today, the festival includes fourteen stages that over the years have featured a who's who of country superstars, including Dolly Parton, Willie Nelson, Earl Scruggs, Alison Krauss and Union Station, Emmylou Harris, Randy Travis, Lyle Lovett, and Vince Gill.

In 2011 more than seventy-eight thousand people attended MerleFest. For the parking lot pickers, there were guitar, banjo, and mandolin contests, as well as songwriting showcases. In addition to bringing more than $12 million to the local economy, this bluegrass paradise distributes millions of dollars to civic and charitable organizations.

When renowned folklorist Ralph Rinzler heard Watson play, he immediately began booking him at festivals and folk clubs, such as Gerde's Folk City in New York's Greenwich Village. In 1963 Watson landed a coveted spot at the Newport Folk Festival. In later years Watson toured with his son Merle, another hot guitar picker, who died in a tractor accident in 1985.

A Timeless Quality

Although bluegrass is based on ancient British and Irish fiddle tunes, the style was kicked into high gear by Doc Watson, Bill Monroe, Earl Scruggs, and others. What began as simple string band music in the hills and hollows of Appalachia can be heard today throughout the world. While it may be the music of the people, it requires a patient and talented musician to perform the double-quick licks and high, lonesome harmonies true to the style. But there is a sense of joy and wonder—and a timeless quality of an old-fashioned barn dance—wherever the ringing sound of banjos, fiddles, guitars, and mandolins splits the air. Although bluegrass founder Bill Monroe is dead, as biographer Richard D. Smith writes, "This powerful music may go on for centuries. . . . And as long as bluegrass is played, heard, and loved, Mr. Bill Monroe will never have a last day on earth."[16]

CHAPTER 2

Cowboy Music and Western Swing

As the *Grand Ole Opry* made old-time country music a national sensation in the 1930s, another style paralleled its growth. The commercialization of hillbilly music in the record and radio industries provided an avenue for cowboys to bring their western songs to a wider audience. The cowboy music was not "Red River Valley" or "Buffalo Gals." These songs from the nineteenth century were popular when thousands of real cowboys actually worked the plains. Instead, the new cowboy music was a product of the Great Depression, when millions of Americans lost their jobs and lived in grinding poverty. The music and lyrics glorified the romantic concepts of the Wild West cowboy popularized in dime novels and Hollywood movies. As Bill C. Malone explains, songs of heroic cowboys provided a musical link to better times: "The cowboy of popular culture carried little of the grime, sweat, and manure of the cattle kingdom but instead appealed to Americans as fearless, independent, moral, and a White Knight of the Plains."[17]

Real Singing Cowboys

In the 1930s there were dozens of cowboy bands with names like the Lonesome Cowboys, the Sons of the Pioneers, Cowboy Slim, and the Girls of the Golden West. Many of these groups consisted of professional musicians taking advantage of the demand for cowboy acts. Most never roped a steer or mended a fence. For example, the Sons of the Pioneers was led by Leonard Slye, a former factory worker and truck driver who grew up in a crowded, rundown apartment in Cincinnati, Ohio. While in the Sons of the

Harry "Haywire Mac" McClintock

Harry "Haywire Mac" McClintock was a roving song-writer who led a very interesting life, as music journalist Kurt Wolff explains:

> McClintock wasn't your average cowboy singer. He wasn't your average anything, in fact. Born in Knoxville, Tennessee, in 1882, he left home as a teenager to ride the rails and see the world. . . . In addition to making music, he held an assortment of odd jobs during his lifetime, including cowboy, mule driver, seaman and journalist. Haywire Mac, a nickname he picked up along the way, recorded more than forty sides for Victor, but he became well known as a pioneering radio personality. . . .
>
> Mac's hobo songs were gritty and unflinching on the one hand, yet also presented a good-natured view of the wanderer's lifestyle—which was a common experience at the time, as many young men rode the rails both as a way to see the world and as a means to travel between jobs. ["Hallelujah, Bum Again"] isn't so much a ballad on the perils of homelessness as it is a celebration of the hobo lifestyle—something the protagonist has adopted by choice. "I don't like work, and work don't like me," sings McClintock, "and that is the reason I'm so hungry."

Kurt Wolff. *Country Music: The Rough Guide.* London: Rough Guides, 2000, pp. 55–56.

Pioneers, Slye had hits with cowboy songs like "Cool Water" and "Tumbling Tumbleweeds." (Both songs were written in 1936 by Bob Nolan, a Canadian.) Slye changed his name to Roy Rogers in 1938 and starred in a string of hit movies that made him the most famous singing cowboy in the world.

Unlike Roy Rogers, Jules Verne Allen, who billed himself as Longhorn Luke, was a real cowboy. As a young man Allen worked on a cattle ranch in Waxahachie, Texas. He later became a broncobuster—someone who breaks wild horses to the saddle—in Montana. Throughout the 1930s Allen performed on radio stations throughout the West, singing songs about his life as a roughrider. Longhorn Luke recorded "The Cowtrail to Mexico," "Little Joe, the Wrangler," and "The Cowboy's Dream," songs that popularized cowboy music throughout the United States.

Goebel Reeves, aka the Texas Drifter, was another cowboy who sang from experience. Although his father was in the Texas legislature, Reeves left his pampered life to ride the rails as a hobo. Like other drifters during the Depression, Reeves encountered hunger, isolation, brutal railroad detectives, and cold prison cells. This lent a genuine voice to the songs he wrote, including "Hobo's Lullaby," "The Cowboy's Prayer," and "The Hobo and the Cop."

The hard-traveling tradition was shared by other country singers at the time. Cliff Carlisle described his experiences in hits such as "Hobo Jack's Last Ride," "Box Car Blues," and "Just a Lonely Hobo." Harry McClintock, nicknamed Haywire Mac, was a rover who wrote the classics "Hallelujah, Bum Again," "Jesse James," "Texas Rangers," and "Goodbye Old Paint."

Hollywood Cowboys

Hollywood film directors were quick to pick up on the singing cowboy trend. The first genuine horse-riding balladeer to appear on the silver screen was trick rider Ken Maynard, who sang traditional trailside songs such as "The Lone Star Trail."

Gene Autry, the superstar of the singing cowboys, was originally a telegraph operator for the railroad in Sapupla,

Gene Autry, seen here with his horse Champion, was a world famous "singing cowboy" and movie star in the 1930s and 1940s.

Oklahoma. Autry's claim to fame was that he could closely imitate Jimmie Rodgers' yodeling style. Autry lost his office job when the Depression hit in 1929, which prompted him to ride the rails to New York City. He walked up and down the busy streets with his guitar, visiting record companies and begging executives for auditions.

Autry finally recorded an album for Victor Records titled *Oklahoma's Singing Cowboy*, which landed him a spot on the influential WLS *National Barn Dance* radio show in Chicago. Autry became an overnight sensation, and by 1934 he was in Hollywood making movies, billed as the "Nation's Number One Singing Cowboy."[18] Autry eventually made

The Steel Slide Guitar

The signature sound of western swing is the steel guitar, an instrument developed in Hawaii during the nineteenth century. Indigenous Hawaiian musicians were fascinated with the oceanlike sound that could be produced by the slide guitar when the slide bar was moved up and down the strings. The original steel guitar has eight strings and is sometimes called a lap steel because it is played while resting in the musician's lap. By the mid-1930s the steel guitar, electrified and played through a guitar amp, had moved to the mainland. Popularized by Leon McAuliffe, of the Texas Playboys, the steel guitar became a fixture in country bands.

The steel guitar eventually expanded into several other styles after additional strings were added. Because the guitars used fixed tunings, players added another neck tuned to a different key, which allowed them more versatility. The second neck made the guitars heavier, so thin metal legs were added, making the lap steel a "table steel." Finally, pedals and knee levers were attached, creating what is called the pedal steel guitar. When one of the pedals is depressed by the player's foot, it raises the pitch of an individual string. Moving the knee lever lowers the pitch. This gives the pedal steel a unique twang closely associated with country music.

more than a hundred films and became the most famous singing cowboy in the world. As Bill C. Malone writes:

> While becoming one of the most popular and wealthy actors in Hollywood, Autry also created the stereotype of the heroic cowboy who was equally adept with a gun and guitar. . . . With Autry ensconced as a singing movie cowboy, hillbilly music now had a new medium through which to popularize itself. The Silver Screen romanticized the cowboy and helped to shape the public idea of western music.[19]

Autry's influence was immense, and Hollywood producers began searching for other cowboy acts. Dozens of country bands searching for fame dropped their traditional hillbilly repertoire, bought cowboy outfits, and adopted names such as the Riders of the Purple Sage and the Cowboy Ramblers. Even writers in Tin Pan Alley—an area of New York City that was home to professional composers—who had never been west of New Jersey turned out cowboy hits such as "I'm an Old Cowhand From the Rio Grande" and "Home in Wyoming."

The King of Western Swing

Far from the Hollywood silver screen, in real cowboy country, new elements were showing up in western music. The diverse musical culture of Texas included African American jazz and blues, hoedown fiddles, urban pop, Mexican mariachi, and Louisiana Cajun music. This wide range of sounds came together in western swing music, a mixture sometimes called cowboy jazz, which topped the country charts for nearly twenty years.

Because it embraced so many styles, western swing was played with big bands, some with more than a dozen players. Music in a typical 1930s western swing band might be produced by a piano, mandolin, bass, slide guitars, saxophones, drums, and several fiddles, trumpets, and vocalists. While members of western swing bands usually dressed in cowboy boots and Stetson hats, they were actually playing music that owed more to urban jazz than hillbilly records. The country western flavor was added by the fiddles and pedal steel guitars, along with lyrics about cities such as San Antonio and Amarillo, Texas, and Tulsa, Oklahoma.

Bob Wills, from Turkey, Texas, was the king of western swing. From the age of three, Wills worked side by side in the Texas cotton fields with local black musicians who taught him blues and Dixieland jazz. He played his first gig in 1915 at the age of ten when his fiddling father, John, got drunk and failed to appear at a ranch dance. Young Bob filled in, sawing out the only six songs he knew by heart. The cowpokes, ranch hands, and assembled ladies first laughed at the small boy, but soon started dancing.

By the time he was twenty-five, Wills was pioneering "western jazz"— intermingling his fiddle licks with jazz and blues sounds. In 1930 Wills played regularly on radio shows in Fort Worth, Texas. He soon added singer Milton Brown to his Wills Fiddle Band, a pumped-up string band with fiddles, a piano, banjo player, and two guitarists that utilized dance hall rhythms while trading lightning-fast riffs. In 1932, when the band landed an important gig on a radio program sponsored by Light Crust Flour, Wills and Brown renamed the group the Light Crust Doughboys.

Although the Doughboys were popular, their success was hampered by Wills, who would occasionally disappear on weeklong drinking binges. This caused the band to miss important engagements. These outbreaks with alcoholism were rare—Wills remained sober most of the time. However, on one of those occasions when Wills failed to show up for a radio show, the Doughboys were fired, prompting key band members to quit.

The Musical Brownies

It is quite possible that Bob Wills would have been less famous if one of his main competitors, Milton Brown, had not died in a 1936 car accident, well before reaching his prime. It was Brown, backed by Wills on fiddle, who was the first to record western swing songs—"Nancy Jane" and "Sunbonnet Sue"—under the band name the Fort Worth Doughboys. Brown loved to "holler" humorous phrases during songs. He can be heard exclaiming on "Nancy Jane," "Oh Nancy! . . . Ah ha, she's killing me!"[20]

Shortly after leaving the Doughboys, Brown formed a band he called His Musical Brownies. The group's popularity quickly rivaled that of the Doughboys. The Brownies' sound was boosted by the addition of Bob Dunn, whose electric steel guitar was the first amplified instrument used in country music. Fellow musician Jimmy Thomason recalls how Dunn learned to amplify his guitar while jamming at Coney Island in New York:

> He ran into this black guy who was playing a steel guitar with a homemade pickup attached to it. He had this thing hooked up through an old radio or something and was playing these blues licks. Well, this just knocked Bob out and he got this guy to show him how he was doing it.[21]

When Dunn took the guitar back to Texas, he was the only musician in the state to possess such an instrument.

The guitar amplifier he played through was another high-tech wonder of the day, since the first amps were produced in 1930.

Even without the electric steel guitar, the Brownies made a unique and original sound that Brown called hot-jazz hillbilly string music. Record producers did not fail to notice, and the Brownies recorded more than a hundred songs in four years—producing fifty songs in one marathon recording session in March 1936. Meanwhile, the Brownies were "blowing the roof off" nightclubs and packing in huge crowds, as music journalist Kurt Wolff writes:

> The Brownies' hot, swinging dance music struck a chord with people all over the state who were suffering through the Depression. The music was hot and loose, with a mixture of fiddle, piano and guitar playing, a Dixieland-style rhythm, Dunn's amplified steel and Brown's smooth lead vocals. They played familiar jazz tunes like "St. Louis Blues" . . . and steaming-hot Mexican-flavored numbers like "In El Rancho Grande." At his peak Brown's songs were wild, juicy and almost out of control—the instrumentalists firmly tethered to the rhythm, yet at the same time appearing to barely hang on.[22]

The Brownies's brand of hot western swing came to a tragic end when Milton Brown was killed suddenly in a car accident. While he was alive, the Brownies never gained much fame beyond the Southwest.

"What Makes Bob Holler?"

In 1933, after the Light Crust Doughboys broke up, Bob Wills put together a band he named Bob Wills and His Texas Playboys. It consisted of Wills on fiddle, a vocalist, pianist, bassist, and a rhythm guitarist. Wills also brought in Leon McAuliffe, whose skill with the slide bar on the electric steel guitar is legendary. McAuliffe's 1936 composition "Steel Guitar Rag" helped popularize the steel guitar throughout the United States, making it an essential instrument in country bands.

Between 1934 and 1942 the Texas Playboys worked out

of Tulsa and played a continual series of radio and dance shows. In a 1935 recording session in Dallas, Texas, Wills utilized a thirteen-piece band that included trumpet, saxophone, clarinet, trombone, and a trio of violinists. The fiddle players learned jazz licks from the horn players, and this incarnation of the Texas Playboys was the first to play true to the style that would later be labeled western swing.

In retrospect, the western swing sound seemed musically logical, but at the time the wild sounds generated quite a bit of controversy. For example, the Tulsa musicians union refused membership to the Texas Playboys because union bosses ruled that their sound was not music and by extension, the Playboys were not musicians. Despite this prejudice, the Playboys were some of the hottest—and most entertaining—musicians around.

The music of the Texas Playboys was, above all, dance music. It revolved around the fiddles, but Wills tried to distance himself from the hillbilly label and instead sought to project an air of musical sophistication and class. The band played blues songs such as "Sittin' on Top of the World,"

Bob Wills, on the horse on the right, and His Texas Playboys with their tour bus in 1945. Their music was an eclectic mix of country standards, fiddle tunes, blues, and jazz.

Bob Wills's *For the Last Time*

In 1969 Bob Wills became paralyzed on the right side of his body after suffering a stroke. Sensing his death was near, he decided he wanted to assemble the old Texas Playboys for one more recording session, which took place in December of 1973. The resulting album was a double LP titled *For the Last Time* (later released as a single CD). Although they hadn't played together in thirty years, the Playboys expertly ran through Wills classics such as "Texas Playboy Theme," "What Makes Bob Holler?" "San Antonio Rose," "Bubbles in My Beer," and "Big Balls In Cowtown." They were joined on the vocals by country superstar Merle Haggard, a huge Wills fan since childhood. Meanwhile Wills sat in the middle of the room in his wheelchair, beaming with joy and throwing in an occasional "Ahhhh-ha!"

After six songs, Wills went home. That night he had another stroke and slipped into a coma. The Playboys continued recording, now with new determination to bring the old songs alive again. Wills was still unconscious when *For the Last Time* was released in 1974, but he clung to life until May 1975. Today *For the Last Time* stands as an unshakable testimony to the man who pioneered western swing.

Jimmie Rodgers compositions such as "Blue Yodel No. 1," and jazzy numbers such as "Osage Stomp." Despite this eclectic repertoire, the music was fun, as Kurt Wolff writes:

> For all its sophistication, the Playboys' music was also wild, loose and free of stylistic constraints. When twin fiddles, guitars, horns and drums fired into song, "rowdy" was definitely part of the agenda. The players were superb, and one by one each would take solos that boggled the minds of the spectators and dancers. Western swing was all about fun and good times, and Wills' whoops . . . and interjections of "play that trombone, boy" or "take it away, Leon" when each man stepped to the mike gave the whole experience a playful feeling. . . . Cindy Walker even wrote a song for the Playboys titled "What Makes Bob Holler?" that poked gentle fun at Wills' uninhibited commentary; it became a Playboys standard.[23]

With an eclectic mix of country standards, fiddle tunes, blues, and jazz, the Texas Playboys' records offer something for everyone. By 1940 the Texas Playboys were competing with popular jazz-based swing bands led by Tommy Dorsey, Glenn Miller, and Benny Goodman. That same year the Playboys' song "New San Antonio Rose," about a beautiful Texas maiden, was stocked in more than three hundred thousand jukeboxes—coin-operated phonographs that allowed listeners to hear their favorite songs for a nickel. The song went on to sell a million copies. Other early forties Playboys hits included "Take Me Back to Tulsa," "Ida Red," and "Let's Ride With Bob."

Like many other singing cowboys, Wills soon made it out to Hollywood, where his entire band appeared in the 1941 film *Go West, Young Lady.* The next year Wills was hired by Columbia Pictures to appear in eight films.

By the late 1940s Wills was the highest-paid leader of any band in the country. In 1947 he opened his own nightclub, Wills Point, in Sacramento, California. His live shows from the venue were broadcast on the radio and heard throughout the West. When the Playboys put on shows in Washington, Oregon, California, Texas, and Arizona, they drew up to ten thousand people a night—huge crowds for that era.

Rhythm by Another Name

In the early 1950s Bob Wills' fortunes began to fade. His music was considered too sophisticated for postwar country fans and too country for pop music radio stations. The popularity of western swing took another hit in the mid-1950s when Elvis Presley, Chuck Berry, Jerry Lee Lewis, and Bill Haley & His Comets burst onto the scene. These artists combined country "hillbilly" sounds with fast-tempo rhythm and blues to create a new style called rockabilly.

Rockabilly, popularized by white musicians with country music backgrounds, was a style of rock and roll pioneered in the late 1940s by Wynonie Harris and other African American musicians. Harris songs like "Good Rockin' Tonight," with its shouted vocals, loud hand claps, rollick-

ing piano, and walking bass line, are credited as some of the first rock-and-roll songs.

When American teenagers began buying millions of rock-and-roll and rockabilly records, western swing was all but forgotten. This caused Wills great heartache. He felt his music, which combined country, blues, and jazz music, laid the foundation for the rock-and-roll revolution. As he told a Tulsa newspaper in 1957:

> Rock and Roll? Why, man, that's the same kind of music we've been playin' since 1928! . . . We didn't call it rock and roll back when we introduced it as our style back in 1928, and we don't call it rock and roll the way we play it now. But it's just basic rhythm and has gone by a lot of different names in my time. It's the same, whether you just follow a drum beat like in Africa or

In the mid 1950s, performers such as Chuck Berry combined country music with fast-tempo rhythm and blues into a new style called rockabilly.

Rock and Roll and Rockabilly

In 1955 the innovative guitarist and songwriter Chuck Berry had a number-one hit with the song "Maybelline." Berry freely admitted that the loping dance beat of the song was based on "Ida Red," a 1938 hit for Bob Wills and His Texas Playboys. Like many other early rock songs, "Maybelline" combined country with African American boogie-woogie, which features a driving rhythm that originated in black churches. The new sound was called rockabilly, one of the earliest types of rock and roll.

In a way, rockabilly was the opposite of western swing music. Rockabilly lacked tight arrangements and sophisticated musicianship. While swing bands utilized dozens of virtuoso musicians playing advanced jazz licks, rockabilly groups needed nothing more than a singer accompanied by a stand-up "slap" bass, an electric guitar, and a drummer. The exciting new beat of rockabilly was behind early Elvis Presley hits like "Blue Suede Shoes" and propelled artists like Gene Vincent and Jerry Lee Lewis to the top of the charts in the second half of the 1950s.

surround it with a lot of instruments. The rhythm's what's important.[24]

Wills continued to play on occasion, but his declining health in the early 1960s forced him to break up his band. A stroke in 1969 paralyzed his right side and left him unable to play. The pioneer of country swing died in 1975.

Melting Pot Music

While Bob Wills and Milton Brown pioneered the sounds of western swing, they were joined by others, including two of Bob's brothers, Billy Jack Wills and Johnnie Lee Wills, both of whom performed and recorded in the shadow of their famous brother. Fiddler Spade Cooley made a name for himself leading a large swing band in Southern California. Cooley's band

perfected a smoother, more polished sound using written musical arrangements as opposed to improvised jazz licks.

Other names from western swing's golden years included Tex Williams, a former vocalist with Cooley, and Pee Wee King and His Golden West Cowboys, who scored a huge hit with "Tennessee Waltz." Pee Wee King was not a cowboy, however, but an accordion player raised on polka music in Milwaukee, Wisconsin.

Western swing might have passed into oblivion if not for a 1970s revival of the style by the group Asleep at the Wheel. The band recorded many well-received albums that revived Bob Wills standards such as "Take Me Back to Tulsa" and "Hubbin' It" for baby boomers raised on rock. The band also created its own original western swing classics such as "Let Me Go Home Whiskey," "Bump Bounce Boogie," and

Spade Cooley, standing left, created a smoother, more polished western swing sound with his band in Southern California.

"Miles and Miles of Texas." Asleep at the Wheel continued to keep western swing alive well into the twenty-first century.

While some of the most talented musicians around played western swing, they never took themselves too seriously. The music always had a joyous and often humorous feel, from Bob Wills hollering out his witty asides, to amusing song titles such as "Boot Scootin' Boogie." With its distinctive blend of blues, jazz, country, Mexican, and Cajun sounds, western swing is music that could only have been invented in the melting pot of the United States.

CHAPTER 3

Honky-Tonk Music

From its earliest days, country music was about rambling, whether it was on trains, horses, or on foot. During the Depression in the 1930s, country music took to the road, as millions of Americans crisscrossed the nation's highways in search of work. Some traveled to work in the orchards of California, while others rattled on down to the oil fields of Texas and Oklahoma.

America was on the move, and many of the rambling workers were displaced Southerners. They brought their country music with them to small rough-and-tumble bars and roadhouses called honky-tonks that sprang up on the sides of major highways. Whether they were located outside Tulsa, Oklahoma; Houston, Texas; or Los Angeles, California; honky-tonks were places where patrons could drink, dance, complain, and find love after a tough day at a hard job.

Some honky-tonks had dance floors and live entertainment; others featured jukeboxes. After a hard day at work, barely scraping by on their small paychecks and missing their loved ones, honky-tonk patrons did not want to hear old-time country records with their quaint stories or religious messages. They wanted songs that spoke to their own personal joys and sorrows, and fame and fortune awaited those singers and songwriters who could sing to the honky-tonkers in their own language.

"Ball-Heads, Bachelors and Leading Citizens"

The term *honky-tonk* was coined in the late nineteenth century to describe the rowdy taverns that lined the trails of Texas, Oklahoma, and other Southwest locales. The first published appearance of the word *honky-tonk* can be traced to an 1894 newspaper in Ardmore, Oklahoma, a town about twenty miles from the Texas border. In the *Daily Ardmorite,* a journalist wrote on the front page that "the honk-a-tonk last night was well attended by ball-heads, bachelors and leading citizens." While it is unclear today who or what ball-heads might have been, it is certain that more than a century ago the term was familiar to the rural folks in that corner of Oklahoma.

It was also obvious that songwriters and musicians were quite familiar with honky-tonks. In 1916 Victor Records released a song called "Honky Tonky." In 1918 a New York musical called *Everything* contained the gem "Everything Is Hunky Dory Down in Honky Tonk Town." By the 1920s a flood of songs used the term, including "Sister Honky Tonk" and "Honky Tonk Train Blues." By the end of the decade, the term *honky-tonk* had entered the literary world, having been used in a poem by Carl Sandburg and mentioned in novels by John Steinbeck and William Faulkner.

Quoted in Nick Tosches. *Country: The Twisted Roots of Rock 'n' Roll.* New York: De Capo Press, 1996, p. 26.

Oil Field Roughnecks

Most honky-tonks were housed in hastily constructed buildings on the long, lonely highways of the Southwest. They were often built a few miles outside of town, on "the wrong side of the tracks," because people in respectable neighborhoods would not tolerate the roughnecks who gathered at these establishments.

In Texas and Oklahoma, the honky-tonk clientele consisted of oil field workers. These laborers were mainly single young men who flocked to boomtowns when oil was discovered and moved on when the wells ran dry. After working grueling twelve-hour shifts, they slept in hotels, tents, truck beds, and even under pool tables in honky-tonks. When Saturday night came, the crowd was usually ready for some hard drinking. Far from their wives and girlfriends, the drunk and disheartened men often ended up fighting with fists, knives, and occasionally guns. For this reason, honky-tonks were often called bloodbuckets. Singer Floyd Tillman remembers playing some of the rougher Texas honky-tonks, "where you had to dodge [thrown] beer bottles, and when the fights broke out you were supposed to speed it up and play the music real fast."[25]

"Girls Jump in Cars"

Al Dexter was familiar with the honky-tonk world—the songwriter owned the Round-Up Club in Turnertown, Texas. However, in 1936, when his songwriting partner James B. Paris suggested they pen a tune using the word *honky-tonk*, Dexter claimed he was unfamiliar with the phrase. As Dexter told music journalist Nick Tosches:

> One day I went to see [James] Paris . . . and he said, "I thought of a title last night that'll set the woods on fire." I asked him what it was, and he said, "Honky Tonk Blues." I asked him where he got that idea. I never heard the word, so I said, "What is a honky-tonk?" So he said, "These beer joints up and down the road where the girls jump in cars and so on." I said, "Never thought about it like that." He said, "Use your thinker-upper [brain] and let's write a song like that."[26]

Apparently Paris had put a good idea in Dexter's "thinker-upper," because the song "Honky Tonk Blues" helped define the music style that would remain popular well into the twenty-first century. While Dexter sings about the blues he can't lose because of his honky-tonk girl, two electric guitars create a rhythm like a Model A Ford bouncing rapidly down the highway. The lead guitar break combines hot single-note picking over jazz chords that give the feel of the warm Texas breeze. And unlike the acoustic instruments of old-time music, the recorded sounds of the electric bass and amplified guitars were perfect for cutting through the noisy din of the boisterous honky-tonks. "Honky Tonk Blues" was a major hit, and within a few years even staunch music traditionalists like Roy Acuff were performing numbers such as "Honky Tonk Mamas."

Ernest Tubb, who had the first million-selling honky-tonk hit in 1941, performs during the Grand Ole Opry broadcast in 1956.

Ernest Tubb Recasts Honky-Tonk

One of the biggest honky-tonk stars of the 1940s, Ernest Tubb, was born in 1914 in Crisp, Texas—about forty miles from Dallas. During the early part of his career Tubb imitated Jimmie Rodgers, whose Depression-era songs about Texas, railroad trains, and the homesick blues inspired a later generation of honky-tonkers.

Tubb was only nineteen years old when Rodgers died in 1933, but the Texas singer befriended the Singing Brakeman's widow, Carrie. She liked Tubb's style and loaned the lanky singer Rodgers's suit coat for early photographs and, more important, his sweet-sounding Martin guitar for recording sessions. Tubb's early imitations of Rodgers did not sell, but the singer owned his own honky-tonk called the E&E Tavern. Tubb heard honky-tonk music on the jukebox, but felt that most of it was performed without heart and soul. This led Tubb to find his own style based on sensibilities he learned from Rodgers. As Nick Tosches explains:

> If Rodgers had taught [Tubb] anything, it was that music without power—be it the power of meanness, the power of love, the power of sentimentality, the power of sadness or madness, sweetness or venom—was music without worth. Ernest Tubb was on his way to empowering country music and recasting honky-tonk with his own new-found voice, a voice that was the sum of all he had learned from the master, and from himself. And he was on his way to glory.[27]

In 1941 Tubb recorded "Walking the Floor Over You," and it became the first million-selling honky-tonk hit. The song was also the first country "crossover" hit—it sold to both country and mainstream pop music audiences. Tubb, who had been struggling in the music business for years, became an "overnight sensation," taking honk-tonk music to the stage of the Grand Ole Opry and appearing in a few Hollywood movies. He continued to score hits with "Drivin' Nails in My Coffin" and "Let's Say Goodbye Like We Said Hello," songs considered today as honky-tonk classics.

Honky-Tonk Everywhere

America entered World War II in December 1941, and the Texas honky-tonks began to empty as millions of men joined the military. The music remained vibrant, however, as honky-tonk stars such as Ernest Tubb played USO (United Service Organizations, Inc.) tours for military personnel. These shows, held both in the United States and overseas, exposed country performers to audiences who had previously ignored or scorned what they referred to as hillbilly music. Country music was so popular that one of its stars even became part of a taunt on the battlefield. United States Marines fighting in Asia reported that Japanese soldiers mocked them by insulting the president, a national baseball hero, and "the King of Country Music," screaming "To hell with Roosevelt! To hell with Babe Ruth! To hell with Roy Acuff!"[28]

On the home front, honky-tonk continued to top the record charts. In 1942 Al Dexter scored his first crossover hit with "Pistol Packin' Mama." The song is about a woman who runs into a bar with a gun to fill her cheating man full of lead. "Pistol Packin' Mama" was on every jukebox in the country and sold even more records than Ernest Tubbs's "Walking the Floor Over You." The song was covered by Bing Crosby and Frank Sinatra, the biggest pop stars of the day.

Honky-Tonkin' in California

With his hit topping the charts, Al Dexter often toured in California, where tens of thousands of Southerners had moved to work in the defense industry. In the San Francisco Bay area alone, 29 percent of the newcomers came from Arkansas, Louisiana, Texas, and Oklahoma. The numbers were similar in Los Angeles and San Diego. To cater to the displaced Southerners, roadside honky-tonks opened near defense plants and military bases. Meanwhile, radio programmers saw gold in honky-tonk, and nearly every major California station featured barn dance shows and honky-tonk music acts.

Merle Travis (right) was known for his unique thumb-picking guitar style called "Travis Picking."

With country "going Hollywood," it was inevitable that performers' clothing would become more glamorous. A Russian tailor named Nutya "Nudie" Cohn aided this process when he opened a shop in his Los Angeles garage. Cohn was one of the first people to sew fake diamonds, called rhinestones, onto western suits. By the end of the decade Cohn had moved to Hollywood, and nearly every honky-tonk singer who could afford it had a shimmering Nudie suit in his wardrobe.

With guitar playing as flashy as a

Rhinestone Cowboys

Journalist Candi Strecker describes the rhinestone-covered Nudie suits popular with honky-tonk performers since the 1940s:

While top business executives prefer subdued gray flannel suits, country music stars have often reached into their closets for something a bit louder—like an electric turquoise suit with matching Stetson [hat] and boots studded with rhinestones and embroidered with big gold coins and dollar bills. These flamboyantly decorated outfits in peacock colors are called "Nudie suits," after Ukrainian-born, Brooklyn-bred tailor [Nudie Cohn], the western-wear specialist best known for creating them.

Serving as both performance costumes and status symbols, Nudie-style suits are typically embroidered, studded, sequined and spangled with motifs big enough to be seen in the back row of any auditorium. The simplest are trimmed with names, initials, or a pattern of musical notes and guitars. Western images such as cactuses, six-shooters, prairie flowers, or arrows and teepees are also popular. Some outfits play off a performer's name: Porter Wagoner's suits are decked out with wagon wheels, Ferlin Husky's with husky dogs. Other costumes plug hit songs. Nudie made . . . a suit covered with locks, keys and prison bars for Webb Pierce when "In The Jailhouse Now" topped the charts. . . . Among his best-known creations are the $10,000 24-karat gold lamé tuxedo worn by Elvis Presley.

Quoted in Kurt Wolff. *Country Music: The Rough Guide.* London: Rough Guides, 2000, p. 194.

Nudie suit, Merle Travis became one of the West Coast's hottest guitar slingers. Travis was born in the heart of Kentucky coal country, and his songs, such as "Sixteen Tons" and "Dark as a Dungeon," are odes to the suffering faced by coal miners. Travis also wrote humorous songs such as "Smoke! Smoke! Smoke! (That Cigarette)," "Divorce Me C.O.D.," and "So Round, So Firm, So Fully Packed." While that alone would have landed him in the Country Music Hall of Fame, Travis was also known for his unique thumb-picking guitar style, now known as Travis picking, in which the thumb plays a steady rhythm of bass notes while the first and second fingers tickle out the melody on the higher strings.

The Wail of Hank Williams

While the honky-tonkers were pioneering their own sound in California, singer-songwriter Hank Williams was making a name for himself appearing on "barn dance" radio shows and touring bloodbucket honky-tonk bars in his native Alabama.

Williams was born into poverty in rural Butler County, Alabama, in 1923. As a young boy, he learned to play music from an African American street musician named Rufus "Tee-Tot" Payne. By the time he was eighteen, Williams was performing his own songs on local radio stations and had put together a band that played Roy Acuff covers.

Williams had a natural singing style like Ernest Tubb, but also had a "tear" in his voice, based on the vocal wail per-

Hank Williams was the first recording artist to use a music publishing company to oversee his artistic development through a system called A&R, which became the standard throughout the music industry.

fected by Acuff. This combination was beloved by fans of honky-tonk music, and Williams was signed in 1946 by the Nashville, Tennessee, music publishing company founded by Roy Acuff and Fred Rose, a successful songwriter. Like other music publishers, Acuff-Rose signed composers to write hit songs, picked artists to record the tunes, promoted the music, and collected a percentage of the profits, called royalties, from sales of the recordings.

Acuff-Rose selected the best songs for Williams, created musical arrangements, booked recording sessions, and hired musicians. This system, called artists and repertoire, or A&R, was created to oversee the artistic development of a recording talent. It was first used for Williams, but A&R would become standard first in Nashville, then throughout the music industry.

Williams likely needed A&R oversight more than most singers. When he was signed by Acuff-Rose at the age of twenty-three, the pain and torment portrayed in his songs was closely paralleled in his daily life. He loved to drink, and he suffered from constant depression. Williams' problems were aggravated by the deep love he felt for his young wife, Audrey Mae Sheppard. Their union was marked by chaos, as Kurt Wolff writes:

> Hank first met . . . Sheppard while he was touring with a medicine show in southern Alabama. A year later they were married, and almost just as quickly the arguing began, usually fueled by Hank's appetite for booze. Drinking was a habit that would land Hank in jail, dry-docked in a sanatorium, and face down in the gutter many times over.[29]

"I'll Never Get Out of This World Alive"

In 1949 Hank Williams went to Nashville to record the 1920s yodeled lament "Lovesick Blues," a song that perfectly encapsulated the pain of his relationship with his wife. The song, which is about crying the blues since his baby went away, was Williams' first big hit. It stayed on the country charts for forty-two weeks and earned the singer a spot on the Grand Ole Opry, where he was warmly received.

Hank Williams's Notebooks

When Hank Williams died on New Year's Day, 1953, at the age of twenty-nine, he left behind dozens of unfinished songs scribbled on napkins, the pages of notebooks, and even on the backs of envelopes. After Williams's death, a stockpile of sixty-six unpublished songs was placed in a fireproof vault in the offices of Acuff-Rose, his music publisher. The songs were all but forgotten until 2002, when company A&R veteran Mary Martin turned some of the unfinished songs over to Bob Dylan, a music legend who was strongly influenced by Williams.

Rather than record the songs himself, Dylan reached out to other singer-songwriters to write music for the lyrics. The project took years, but in 2011 the album *The Lost Notebooks of Hank Williams* was released. The old songs were reanimated by music legends who consider Hank Williams a major influence in their musical careers. They were performed by Dylan and other superstars, including Alan Jackson, Vince Gill, Patty Loveless, Sheryl Crow, Nora Jones, Jacob Dylan, and Lucinda Williams (no relation to Hank). Williams' granddaughter, country singer Holly Williams, also sings on the album. Although Williams wrote the lyrics long ago, his words about heartache, tears, faded love, and the lonesome blues remain timeless.

While Audrey Mae Sheppard could hardly be blamed for distancing herself from the drunken Williams, the singer portrayed himself as a victim. Using his stormy life for songwriting material, he penned a string of classics that included "Cold Cold Heart," "You Win Again," "I'm So Lonesome I Could Cry," and "Your Cheatin' Heart." These songs were hits on the country charts and were recorded by pop artists. All of Williams's fame and fortune meant little to him as he sank into deep depression after Sheppard left him. As Nick Tosches writes:

[By 1952] Hank was in the worst shape of his life, living

in physical and emotional wretchedness at his mother's boardinghouse in Montgomery [Alabama]. He pined for his faithless wife, Miss Audrey, drank, took [the dangerous tranquilizer] chloral hydrate, drank, fell down and cracked his skull, [drank] some more, and wrote "I'll Never Get Out of This World Alive."[30]

In October 1952, while remaining married to "Miss Audrey," Williams married another woman—onstage at the New Orleans Municipal Auditorium, in front of fourteen thousand paying customers. This stunt did little to make him happy, however. On January 1, 1953, Williams died in the back of a limousine on the way to a concert in Canton, Ohio. His death was attributed to an overdose of tranquilizers and alcohol. Although he was only twenty-nine years old, Williams recorded more than two hundred songs during his six-year career.

Williams' miserable existence paved the way for a songwriting legacy that influenced every honky-tonk singer who followed, as Kurt Wolff writes:

Country music was already in the midst of a honky-tonk revolution . . . [but] the music burst its seams, foamed at the mouth, and was never the same beast again. Though Hank was on the surface a raw and untrained singer, he was also an incredibly expressive one, his voice yipping, breaking, moaning and almost choking on each word, big or small. Locked into each crack and dip of his southern twang was a beauty and truth, pure and very real. . . . Never had pain and sadness sounded so damn good.[31]

Stars who die tragically at the height of their careers often become legends, and Williams is no exception. His personal, introspective songs permanently changed the sound of country and paved the way for a new generation of honky-tonk singers that included Lefty Frizzell, Webb Pierce, Ray Price, Faron Young, Hank Snow, and George Jones.

Honky-Tonk Angels

Songs about drinking, cheating, and lovesick blues were mostly sung by men in the years leading up to Hank

Williams's death. That changed in the summer of 1952 when Tennessee native Kitty Wells rose to the top of the charts with "It Wasn't God Who Made Honky Tonk Angels." Wells started her career singing backup vocals for her husband, a struggling country artist named Johnnie Wright. At the age of thirty-three, she was about to retire from the music business to be a full-time mother, but a record producer persuaded her to record "Honky Tonk Angels." The song was written in response to the line from honky-tonk star Hank Thompson's song "The Wild Side of Life," in which he sings, "I didn't know God made honky tonk angels / I might have known you'd never make a wife." In her song, Wells responds: "It wasn't God who made honky-tonk angels / As you said in the words of your song / Too many times married men think they're still single / That has caused many a good girl to go wrong."[32]

"Honky Tonk Angels" shot to number one and stayed there for six weeks. Wells went on to record more than a dozen hits in the 1950s and early 1960s, earning her the title "Queen of Country Music." With her success, honky-tonk music had a strong female voice, as country superstar Loretta Lynn says:

First time I heard [Kitty Wells] I thought there was an angel singing. . . . I thought, "Here's a woman telling our point of view of everyday life." You know, women staying home at night while the guy's going out for a card game. Game didn't last all night, but the men did. Men going out with the boys, but they're not out with the boys. It was something nobody else was writing or singing about. . . . So I started writing songs.[33]

Patsy Cline's Emotional Essays

After "Honky Tonk Angels" became a hit, Nashville producers were eager to find another female vocalist who could match Kitty Wells's success. They found one in Patsy Cline, a hard-drinking, rowdy hell-raiser who was a true honky-tonk angel. She started learning about the world at the age of sixteen singing in dingy bars.

Cline's first success came in 1957 after she sang "Walkin'

CRAZY

Back In Baby's Arms

Faded Love

YOU'RE STRONGER THAN ME

Sweet Dreams

Walking After Midnight

STRANGE

I FALL TO PIECES

So Wrong

Leavin' On Your Mind

She's Got You

WHY CAN'T HE BE YOU

Patsy Cline died at the height of her career in a private airplane crash in 1963.

After Midnight" on the popular television show *Arthur Godfrey's Talent Scouts,* the *American Idol* of its day. In 1960 Cline's "I Fall to Pieces" went to number one on the country charts and crossed over to the pop charts, rising to number twelve. Cline's singing could grab the attention of any listener, as Nick Tosches writes: "Her voice was a big, astounding thing, capable of yodeling merrily, growling the blues, sobbing with emotion, and vaulting octaves with ease. She could transform even second-rate material into emotional essays."[34]

Like Hank Williams, Cline died tragically at the height of her career, but not from self-destructive behavior. On March 5, 1963, while returning home from a concert, Cline's private plane crashed in bad weather in Tennessee. Cline continues to live on in her music, which has influenced countless female country, pop, and rock vocalists throughout the years.

Cline, Williams, and Wells are the best-known heroes from the heyday of honky-tonk, but there are many others.

Floyd Tillman, Red Foley, Jean Shepard, and others too numerous to name helped make the distinct sound of honky-tonk a lasting style. While the music was based on simple melodies, the emotional and sometimes tragic lives of the singers gave the songs true meaning. Today honky-tonk is one of the major enduring styles of country music. And as long as there are broken hearts, lonesome highways, and honky-tonk bars, the music will remain as vital as it was in the 1940s and 1950s.

CHAPTER 4

The Nashville Sound

In the second half of the 1950s, the sounds of rock and roll were booming out of nearly every radio, record player, and jukebox in the country. Some of the biggest rock stars—Elvis Presley, Jerry Lee Lewis, Gene Vincent, and Buddy Holly—were Southern boys raised on honky-tonk and old-time music.

During this era, Presley, Vincent, and several others recorded in Nashville, Tennessee, and the city's music establishment embraced rock's rising stars. The popular singers were viewed as country acts who happened to appeal to teenagers. This sentiment was on display in a 1957 article in the music industry magazine *Music Reporter*. Editor Charles Lamb wrote that Nashville reigned supreme "on the national music throne by virtue of the undisputed dominance of rock music, produced by one-time country singers to whom the style comes as naturally as breathing."[35]

At the time, Lamb was correct. Early rock and roll helped establish Nashville as the center of the nation's country music and rock recording industry. It soon became apparent, however, that Elvis, Gene, and Jerry Lee were a disaster for country music. When Nashville producers tried to cater to the tastes of teenagers with rock music, they ignored the traditional country audience, which was largely white, working-class, and middle-aged. While alienating their traditional audience, Nashville producers led millions of Southern teenagers to abandon country music. Many of these young adults felt the music had nothing new to say to them, and the sales of country records plummeted.

The dramatic impact of rock on audiences could be clearly seen at the Ryman Auditorium where the Grand Ole Opry is held every Saturday night. From the mid-1920s until 1954, the show was sold out nearly every weekend. By 1958 the auditorium was often more than half empty at showtime. And as steel player Joe Talbot states, it was rock and roll that hurt the Opry:

> I really hate to admit this now, but I hated rock 'n' roll because it killed country music. . . . I mean, it just wiped it out. The audience liked the dance beat, the humor, the energy, the simplicity, the excitement of Elvis Presley. These people put on tremendous shows. I think that's one of the big things that caused our audience to move to rock 'n' roll.[36]

Changes in Radio

Rapid changes in the musical tastes of the public also caused upheaval in the broadcast industry. In 1957 NBC canceled the *Grand Ole Opry* radio show, and in 1960 Chicago's WLS dropped *National Barn Dance*. Both were forced to struggle along on local stations. Changes in radio programming also impacted country music sales. After World War II, as the number of radio stations grew nationwide, station managers implemented a new concept called Top 40. Rather than play music to fit local tastes, programmers picked forty top-selling records, which were played over and over. By the late 1950s rock and roll dominated Top 40 radio. This caused hundreds of country stations to switch over to the Top 40 format. In 1961 there were only 81 full-time country stations left in the United States, down from 650 in 1949.

The booming popularity of television also aggravated radio broadcasters' problems. Although commercial television was not introduced until the late 1940s, by 1955 more than half of the homes in the country had a television. This caused millions of people to abandon their radios. It was hard times in the country music industry, and musicians and executives were desperate to regain their former fortunes.

Nashville Countrypolitan

In 1958 country music executives formed the Country Music Association (CMA) to promote the financial interests of their industry. That meant getting more country radio stations on the air and convincing advertisers that the millions of white, middle-aged people who were still "country" were an important segment of the buying public. The old-time, bluegrass, and honky-tonk that had made earlier country music so successful was seen as no longer fashionable. A consultant for the CMA issued a memo meant to distance country music from the stereotypical hillbilly sounds of previous decades:

> Modern country music has no relationship to rural or mountain life. It is the music of this Nation, of this country, the music of the people. You find no screech fiddles, no twangy guitars, no mournful nasal twangs in the modern Nashville sound of country music.[37]

While the CMA did its part to promote country music, several key record producers worked to rid country of "screech fiddles" and "twangy guitars." Owen Bradley, Don Law, and guitar virtuoso Chet Atkins, producing for Decca, Columbia, and RCA respectively, were responsible for the changes. The producers softened and sweetened country's rougher sounds by muting the steel guitar and banning fiddle breaks and nasal hillbilly singing. The new style featured smooth country crooners backed by gospel-like choruses and lush string arrangements provided by the Nashville Symphony Orchestra. The sounds were relaxed, the beat was easygoing, and the feel was the exact opposite of the jittery noise made by rock and rollers.

The new brand of country music was known as country pop, countrypolitan, or the Nashville sound. Most lyrics were written by a few proven songwriters. Felice and Boudleaux Bryant, a husband-and-wife team, wrote chart toppers such as "Love Hurts" and "Richest Man in the World" in addition to the Everly Brothers's hits "Bye Bye

Love" and "Wake Up Little Susie." Cindy Walker penned the countrypolitan hits "You Don't Know Me," sung by Eddy Arnold, and "Distant Drums," a hit for Jim Reeves. Harlan Howard was another renowned songwriter who composed "I Fall to Pieces," made famous by Patsy Cline, and "Tiger by the Tail," a chart topper for Buck Owens, the king of the Bakersfield, California, country sound.

At countrypolitan recording sessions, instrumentation was supplied by an exclusive group of talented session musicians. They appeared, often without credit, on thousands of records. The basic countrypolitan session band of the

The Bakersfield Sound

In the early 1960s a new sound emerged in Bakersfield, California, that was meant to challenge the countrypolitan sound popular in Nashville. The "Bakersfield sound" was notable for its twangy "chicken picking" guitar style, rock rhythms, and gliding pedal steel licks. The king of the Bakersfield sound was the Texas-born Buck Owens. In 1956 Owens made his first records for Capitol Records in Los Angeles with his band, the Buckaroos. Rather than play the cry-in-your-beer honky-tonk style popularized by Hank Williams, Owens ripped it up with fast rock rhythms, backed by lead player Don Rich on his electric Fender Telecaster. Owens had a string of hits beginning with 1963's "Act Naturally," later covered by the Beatles. After that breakthrough, Owens compiled twenty number-one hits on the country charts before 1972.

Although he achieved international fame, Owens refused to abandon Bakersfield, which was soon nicknamed Buckersfield. In 1996 Owens turned his adopted hometown into a tourist attraction, opening the Buck Owens Crystal Palace, a $7 million museum, concert hall, and restaurant. Although he died in 2006, Buck Owens and the Bakersfield sound continue to influence country music in the twenty-first century.

1960s consisted of Grady Martin on guitar, Roy Huskey Jr. on bass, Floyd Cramer or Hargus "Pig" Robbins on piano, Charlie McCoy on harmonica, and Buddy Harmon on drums. Background vocals on countless Nashville recordings were provided by the Anita Kerr Singers. In addition to leading her vocal group, Kerr provided arrangements on many recordings. She was also one of the only women hired to produce for RCA in the 1960s.

Country Crooners

While writers, producers, and session musicians labored behind the scenes, the stars of the Nashville sound were the singers whose faces and names appeared on the record sleeves. The first official countrypolitan hits were Don Gibson's 1958 "Oh Lonesome Me" / "I Can't Stop Loving You," both produced by Chet Atkins. The mournful songs were both written by the singer—on the same day. Gibson was known as the Sad Poet because he wrote so many hits about heartbreak and loneliness, but his clear, melodious singing voice came to define country crooners of the era.

"Gentleman" Jim Reeves was another velvet-voiced singer who embodied the Nashville sound. Born in Texas in 1923, Reeves began his career in 1952, filling in for Hank Williams when the honky-tonk superstar was drunk and failed to appear on *Louisiana Hayride*. In 1959 Reeves scored a major hit with "He'll Have to Go." The song begins with the memorable line "put your sweet lips closer to the phone," sung over a muted musical backdrop. During the early 1960s, Reeves dominated the country charts with slow, gospel-tinged songs such as "Guilty" and "Welcome to My World." Reeves loved to fly his own airplane to gigs; when his small plane crashed in 1964, the beloved singer was killed instantly. By dying at the height of his career, the singer went on to achieve cult status. He was inducted into the Country Music Hall of Fame in 1967.

The Thin Man from West Plains

Porter Wagoner, born in 1927 in the Ozark Mountains, had a long and bountiful country career. Known as the Thin

Chet Atkins

Chet Atkins was a guitarist whose extraordinary four-finger picking style made him one of the most notable musicians of the twentieth century—in every musical category. Atkins began producing for RCA in Nashville in 1952 and took over as head of the A&R division in 1960. In this role he influenced the sounds of country superstars such as Eddy Arnold, Jim Reeves, Waylon Jennings, Charley Pride, and Dolly Parton.

Atkins was the chief architect of the smooth Nashville country sound, meant to make the music "countrypolitan," or more appealing to listeners in suburbs and "uptown" metropolitan, or big city, areas. Although these production techniques attracted more listeners and improved the fortunes of the country music

Chet Atkins was the chief architect of the smooth Nashville country sound or "countrypolitan."

industry, many criticized the slick, less traditional sound. Atkins himself had mixed feelings about his success as he told an interviewer in 1976: "I hate to see country going uptown. . . .We're about to lose our identity and get all mixed up with other music. . . . Of course, I had a lot to do with changing country, and I do apologize. We did it to broaden the appeal, and to keep making records different, to surprise the public."

Quoted in Joli Jensen. *Nashville Sound: Authenticity, Commercialization, and Country Music.* Nashville: Vanderbilt University, 1998, p. 119.

Man from West Plains (Missouri), Wagoner began his career singing in honky-tonks. His flamboyant style included blond hair styled in an inflated pompadour and outrageous, shimmering Nudie suits.

Wagoner's first number-one hit, "A Satisfied Mind," made him a national star in 1955, and he was a regular at the Opry by 1957. Throughout his career Wagoner mixed the straight-ahead honky-tonk style with the Nashville sound, making sure the strings and choruses did not dilute the true country edge. But the words of his hit songs—such as "I've Enjoyed as Much of This as I Can Stand," "Cold Dark Waters," "Green, Green Grass of Home," and "The Cold Hard Facts of Life"—demonstrate the sentimentality often found in country pop.

The flashy singer achieved national acclaim in 1960 with his own TV program, *The Porter Wagoner Show,* which featured corny jokes and country music. Wagoner was backed on TV by a pair of what he called "gal singers," Norma Jean and Dolly Parton, both of whom became stars in their own right. Parton and Wagoner went on to record several best-selling albums together and had a string of number-one hits between 1967 and 1973. Although the Wagoner-Parton partnership dissolved, the beautiful, harmonious duets they produced are considered pure country gold.

Dolly Parton's Rags to Riches

Once she embarked on a solo career in 1973, Dolly Parton was quickly recognized for her songwriting talents, singing ability, attractive persona, and sharp business sense. Parton, born in 1946, has true country roots, and her early life reads like lyrics from an old-timey song. She was the eighth of twelve children born to a poverty-stricken couple who lived in a cabin in the Smoky Mountains of Tennessee. Like so many others, she was inspired by the music she heard in church and the songs she sang with her family. When she was fourteen, Parton's uncle took her to Nashville, where she recorded an original song titled "Puppy Love." By the time she graduated high school in 1964, she was writing hit songs for other artists.

In 1967 Parton began writing songs that showed a strong, feminist side not found in any style of music before the mid-1970s. Kurt Wolff describes the ironically titled song "Dumb Blonde" as "a take-no-punches song about smashing sexist stereotypes. Like other songs soon to come ('Just Because I'm a Woman' [and] 'When Possession Gets Too

Strong') . . . it revealed a young woman unafraid to put forward a strong female perspective."[38]

Parton also painted a realistic picture of her dirt-poor childhood and the hardships she overcame in songs such as "Coat of Many Colors," "To Daddy," and "In the Good Old Days (When Times Were Bad)." By the late 1970s, Parton had transcended the role of country music singer to become a movie star and a superstar with a broad, mainstream fan base. In 1986 she opened a theme park called Dollywood, modeled on her life. The park attracted more than a million visitors the first year, and by 2010, average attendance was more than double that number.

The Coal Miner's Daughter

Loretta Lynn was another woman of country music who used autobiographical material to write hit songs. Like Dolly Parton's, Lynn's life was one of struggle and hardship followed by fame and fortune. She was born in 1935 in isolated Butcher Holler, Kentucky, where her father struggled to provide for his family, laboring for little pay in the local coal mines. Loretta was only thirteen when she married Oliver Lynn Jr. By the time she was eighteen, she had four children. Lynn was a grandmother at the age of twenty-nine.

Despite a busy family life and a stormy marriage, Lynn aspired to become a singing star. In 1960 she recorded her first single, "I'm a Honky Tonk Girl," which launched her career. Lynn touched the hearts of average country men and women with songs about her life and the world around her. She wrote about honky-tonks, coal mines, drunks, cheating husbands, and backstabbing women. Songs such as "Don't Come Home a Drinkin' (with Lovin' on Your Mind)," "Who's Gonna Take the Garbage Out," and "Your Squaw Is on the Warpath" sum up the rough and tough attitudes of this country star.

In a segment of the music industry aimed at a largely conservative country audience, Lynn often created controversy

Dolly Parton's songs show a strong, feminist point of view.

Some of Loretta Lynn's songs were so controversial that they were banned from country radio in the 1960s and 1970s.

with her honest subject matter. Some of her songs were even banned from country radio. "Dear Uncle Sam," released in 1966 at the height of the Vietnam War, was written from the perspective of a wife whose husband was a soldier killed in the war. Lynn's 1970 hit "Wings Upon Your Horns" is about an innocent country girl, an angel, seduced then abandoned by a devil man. Lynn created the most controversy with the 1972 song "The Pill," a comical song about a woman crediting birth control pills for her newfound freedom.

Despite her coverage of what were considered racy topics at the time, Lynn's honesty, clear vocals, and strong songwriting kept her at the top of the charts. In 1970 she had a number-one hit with the autobiographical "Coal Miner's Daughter," which was also the title of her 1976 autobiography. Lynn's life story was made into a blockbuster movie starring Sissy Spacek in 1980.

Loretta Lynn and Dolly Parton were part of a group of high-spirited, groundbreaking women recording in Nashville in the 1960s. Skeeter Davis, Dottie West, Connie Smith, and Jeannie C. Riley wrote songs of sass, spirit, and sappiness that provided inspiration to countless women who grew up listening to their music.

Epic Ballads and Saga Songs

While countrypolitan dominated the charts, it was not the only sound emanating from Nashville. In the late 1950s there was a folk music revival on college campuses that provided a market for a new type of country music based on the old-time historical ballads. Known as saga or epic music, these songs combined up-tempo beats and slick arrangements with adventure stories.

In 1959 Johnny Horton chalked up the first of these hits with "The Battle of New Orleans." This song is based on the unlikely topic of Andrew Jackson's army beating the British in the War of 1812. Horton followed up with several crossover epic hits, including "North to Alaska," "Sink the Bismarck," and "When It's Springtime in Alaska," before his premature death in a 1960 car accident.

Horton's success inspired Marty Robbins to write "El Paso," a ten-verse number about a cowboy who shoots a rival in a Texas bar because he made a pass at the beautiful dancer Felina. Robbins went on to record a number of cowboy and gunfighter ballads popular throughout the 1960s, including "Big Iron," "The Little Green Valley," and "Saddle Tramp." Other notable Nashville ballads include Jimmy Dean's "Big Bad John," Jim Reeves's "The Blizzard," and Eddy Arnold's "Tennessee Stud."

Nashville Novelties

By 1964 the fad for historical ballads was over, but many remained hungry for memorable country songs that were not sugary countrypolitan productions. Singer-songwriter Roger Miller was a Nashville veteran who was there to provide some novelty and fun. Miller had been in Nashville for years, struggling to get his songs in front of producers and country singers. In the early sixties he had a few minor hits recorded by George Jones and Faron Young, but

Singer-songwriter Roger Miller's clever novelty songs were Grammy Award-winning hits in the 1960s.

Politics and Country Music

In the late 1960s the United States was a divided country. Millions of young people rallied in the streets to protest the war in Vietnam, while much of the older generation supported the conflict. During this era rock radio stations were filled with antiwar songs such as "Eve of Destruction" by Barry McGuire, "Give Peace a Chance" by John Lennon, and "Unknown Soldier" by the Doors. In response to this musical outpouring, largely conservative country singers and songwriters in Nashville fired back with their own songs supporting the war while condemning the protesters.

The most famous country anthem, "Okie From Muskogee," was released by Merle Haggard in 1969, one of the most divisive years of a conflict-ridden decade. Haggard wrote "Okie From Muskogee" after he became disheartened while watching anti-Vietnam War protests on television. The song, which made Haggard a national star, informs listeners that nobody smokes marijuana in Muskogee, Oklahoma, that the flag is still proudly waved, that people don't make a party out of loving, and they don't wear their hair long and shaggy like hippies. Other hit songs protesting the protesters included Dave Dudley's "What We're Fighting For" and Ernest Tubb's "It's America (Love It or Leave It)."

money was scarce. In desperation, Miller decided to record some of his novelty songs himself, borrowing $1,600 to buy studio time.

Miller wrote one of those recorded songs, "Dang Me," in four minutes in a Phoenix, Arizona, hotel room. He was shocked when the song went to number one on the country charts in 1964, soon after crossing over to the pop charts. Miller followed that surprising accomplishment with the hit singles "Chug-a-Lug," "Do Wacka-Do," and his anthem, "King of the Road." In 1965 this success netted Miller five Grammy Awards, with six more the following year.

Miller's success came at a time when the Beatles were

dominating the record charts, along with other British bands such as the Animals, the Rolling Stones, and the Kinks. Even during the pop music era known as the British Invasion, Miller held his own with both country and college crowds. Whoever heard Miller's songs seemed to love his wickedly clever lyrics, tightly honed arrangements, and wacky sense of humor.

Truck Drivin' Men

Miller wasn't the only Nashville singer to ride to the top with a novelty song. In the mid-1960s Dave Dudley firmly wedded country music to big-rig trucks. Dudley was a truck-driving man, and his songs were wildly popular with country audiences. Dudley's most famous tune, "Six Days on the Road," was a million-selling truck-driving anthem covered by everyone from blues artist Taj Mahal to country rockers the Flying Burrito Brothers. A sampling of Dudley's titles, including "There Ain't No Easy Run," "Trucker's Prayer," and "Rolaids, Doan's Pills, and Preparation H," reflect the serious as well as the humorous aspects of propelling an eighteen-wheeler down the road.

Dudley's swaggering singing style has been described as hard-driving and virile. This might have been a polite way of saying he sounded somewhat intoxicated. Dudley's songs like "Truck Drivin' Son of a Gun" and "Two Six Packs Away" were notable for his mumbling vocal delivery and slurred words.

Music City U.S.A.

In the 1960s Nashville earned the nickname Music City U.S.A. and produced songs about semitrucks chugging down the road and heartbreaking ditties filled with luxuriant string arrangements. The promotional efforts of the CMA helped the city retain that title. The idea of country-politan as the "nation's music" was embraced by millions of fans and helped increase the number of country radio stations in the United States to more than two hundred by 1965. (In 2011 there were 1,990 country music stations, making it the most popular radio format in the United States.) The CMA also generated national interest when it opened the Country Music Hall of Fame and instituted the Country Music Awards in 1967.

Today Nashville attracts thousands of hopeful singers, songwriters, and musicians to its famed "Music Row," where all of the major record labels have their offices and studios. From its humble musical beginnings as the hometown of the Grand Ole Opry, Music City U.S.A. has grown to become the creative and financial heart and soul of the country music business.

CHAPTER 5

Country Rock and Outlaws

In the second half of the 1960s Nashville, Tennessee, was known as the country music capital of the world. The people who worked in the city's music industry were also known for promoting conservative political, religious, and social values. To many in Nashville during this era, it seemed as if people in the rest of the country were losing their minds. Beginning around 1966, millions of young people, especially in California and northern cities, began experimenting with marijuana and LSD (lysergic acid diethylamide, or acid). This spawned a period of social upheaval that became known as the counterculture, or hippie movement. Hippies rejected traditional beliefs about politics, sex, and religion. They adopted their own slang and fashions, which included long hair and beards on men, tie-dyed shirts, blue jeans, sandals, and love beads.

Many Nashville residents expressed open contempt for the counterculture. When singer Joni Mitchell visited the city in the late sixties, accompanied by an entourage of West Coast male musicians, she recalled "everybody was hostile to them. People yelled, called them shaggy-hairs and hippies. They felt unsafe."[39] The hippies, in turn, called country music fans *rednecks*, a derogatory term that had replaced *hillbilly* by the 1960s.

Given this hostile environment, many were surprised when Bob Dylan released the album *John Wesley Harding* in 1967. Recorded in Nashville, the album combined Dylan's trademark storytelling lyrics with simple country music. By this time Dylan was one of the most famous singers in the world. He achieved fame in 1963 for protest songs, which addressed issues such as racial inequality, nuclear fallout, and the bomb builders he called masters of war. In 1964 Dylan abandoned what he termed "finger-pointing songs"[40] that made political statements and began writing long epics. Today these influential songs from the mid-1960s, such as "Mr. Tambourine Man," "Gates of Eden," "Just Like a Woman," "Visions Of Johanna," and "Like a Rolling Stone," are considered timeless classics.

Dylan's music made him a hero of the counterculture movement, but his roots were in country music. He was around ten years old in 1951 when he heard Hank Williams on the *Grand Ole Opry* radio show. As he wrote in his 2004 autobiography, "The first time I heard Hank . . . [the] sound of his voice went through me like an electric rod and I managed to get a hold of a few of his [records] . . . and I played them endlessly."[41]

The album *John Wesley Harding* appeared during the height of the hippie era. At this time, many rock musicians were experimenting with the psychedelic drug LSD, which inspired them to create some of the most influential music of the twentieth century. In 1967 rock artists such as Jimi Hendrix, the Grateful Dead, the Beatles, and the Rolling Stones recorded dense musical masterpieces filled with swirling, cascading guitar licks, undulating drums, sound effects, and studio tricks. Dylan's influence was so powerful, however, that the bare country textures of *John Wesley Harding* prompted the Beatles and other top acts to abandon their overproduced sound in an attempt to echo Dylan's musical simplicity.

Nashville Skyline

In April 1969 Bob Dylan followed up *John Wesley Harding* with the album *Nashville Skyline.* It was recorded entirely with Nashville studio musicians and prominently features honky-tonk piano, pedal steel, Dobro, and drums lightly played with brushes instead of drumsticks. On the album, Dylan sings in a low croon rather than the high nasal whine heard on his previous records. In addition, the words to songs like "Peggy Day" and "Country Pie" are simple and direct, more like nursery rhymes than his earlier lyrical epics.

On the songs "One More Night" and "I Threw It All Away," listeners can almost hear Dylan channeling Hank Williams. *Nashville Skyline* also includes "Girl from the North Country," a duet Dylan sings with country legend Johnny Cash. Some of Dylan's fans disapproved of Cash, who was viewed as a redneck. Cash was actually opposed to the Vietnam War, but did not want to alienate his country fans by advertising the fact. The single from the album, "Lay Lady Lay," with its pedal steel and catchy rhythm track played on bongos and a cowbell, was Dylan's biggest hit to date. By the summer of 1969 *Nashville Skyline* was

Bob Dylan on stage at the Isle of Wight Festival on August 31, 1969, the same year he released his "country rock" album Nashville Skyline.

The Legend of Johnny Cash

Johnny Cash is recognized today as a towering legend of country music. He was born in Kingsland, Arkansas, in 1932 and began singing and playing guitar as a young boy. In 1956 Cash had number-one hits with his first two singles for Sun Records: "Folsom Prison Blues" and "I Walk the Line." By the late 1950s Cash was a huge star, but his grueling touring schedule had him playing three hundred shows a year. During this time he was drinking heavily and taking a large number of amphetamines, or "speed." After releasing "Ring of Fire" in 1963, Cash's life spun out of control due to his substance abuse. In 1965 he was arrested in El Paso, Texas, for smuggling drugs; was divorced by his wife, Vivian; and was banned from the Grand Ole Opry.

In 1967, with the help of his future wife June Carter, Cash sobered up. The following year he had a major comeback after the release of the iconic concert album *Johnny Cash at Folsom Prison*. In 1969 Cash had his biggest hit ever with "A Boy Named Sue." That same year he created a TV variety program called *The Johnny Cash Show*, which ran for two years on ABC. In the decades that followed, Cash was known as the Man in Black, was revered as the godfather of country music, and was popular among several generations of country fans. Cash died in 2003 at the age of seventy-one.

Johnny Cash records his iconic concert album Johnny Cash at Folsom Prison *on January 13, 1968.*

the best-selling album in the United States. In the press, Dylan was credited for inventing a new musical style called country rock.

Sweetheart of the Rodeo

Bob Dylan was not the first rock musician to experiment with country sounds, but he was the most successful. Six months before *Nashville Skyline,* the Byrds released what is now considered the first true country rock record, *Sweetheart of the Rodeo.* The Byrds first topped the charts in 1965, covering several Dylan songs including "Mr. Tambourine Man" and "All I Want to Do." By 1967 the group had evolved into a psychedelic rock band with the hit "Eight Miles High," which was banned on many radio stations for its alleged drug references. In 1968 the Byrds attracted the wrath of critics when the group released the album *The Notorious Byrd Brothers.* The record mixed excessive psychedelic studio noise with folk, country, and jazz, sometimes within a single song.

Their career faltering, the Byrds invited the eighteen-year-old Gram Parsons to join the group. Parsons was a wealthy but troubled Georgia native who dropped out of Harvard in 1965. He was strongly influenced by Merle Haggard and George Jones. With Parsons at the helm, the Byrds created *Sweetheart of the Rodeo.* Recorded in Nashville, the album features banjo, pedal steel, and mandolin playing true-to-style bluegrass and honky-tonk. On the album, the Byrds cover the country standards "I Am a Pilgrim" and "You Don't Miss Your Water," along with a few Dylan songs. The album also features Parsons's original country rock songs "Hickory Wind" and "One Hundred Years From Now."

Despite its groundbreaking sound, *Sweetheart of the Rodeo* was not well received. The album only reached number seventy-seven on the *Billboard* Top Album chart. A review in *Rolling Stone* gave the effort faint praise: "The new Byrds do not sound like Buck Owens. . . . They aren't that good. The material they've chosen to record, or rather, the way they perform the material, is simple, relaxed and folky. It's not pretentious, it's pretty. . . . It ought to make the 'Easy Listening' charts."[42] Despite its initial lack of commercial success, *Sweetheart of the Rodeo* went on to inspire an entire generation of country performers.

Gilded Palace of Sin

Due to conflict with other band members, Gram Parsons left the Byrds soon after *Sweetheart of the Rodeo* was released. He quickly formed a new band called the Flying Burrito Brothers with bassist Chris Ethridge, pedal steel player "Sneaky" Pete Kleinow, and the Byrds' former bassist and mandolin player Chris Hillman. In 1969 the pioneering Burrito Brothers' debut album *Gilded Palace of Sin* was released. The majority of songs on the album were written by Parsons working with Hillman and Ethridge.

The cover of *Gilded Palace of Sin* shows the four band members dressed in gaudy Nudie suits, but the group's intention to break tradition is obvious from their custom-made outfits. Parsons's suit is adorned with images of marijuana leaves and mood-altering pills and capsules assumed to be LSD, amphetamines, and barbiturates. While many country artists, including Johnny Cash and George Jones, were pill-popping drug addicts in the 1960s, the public was largely unaware of this fact. The Burrito Brothers seemed to be flaunting their drug use and, for the first time, connecting country music to recreational drugs promoted by the counterculture.

Gilded Palace of Sin only sold sixty thousand copies upon release. After recording a second album, Parsons left the group. The Flying Burrito Brothers carried on without Parsons, but *Gilded Palace of Sin* is considered one of the most influential country rock albums. Keith Richards, guitarist for the Rolling Stones, became one of Parsons' biggest fans. In his 2010 autobiography, Richards describes the effect Parsons's singing had on women: "Even hardened waitresses . . . who heard it all. He could bring tears to their eyes and he could bring that melancholy yearning . . . his effect on women was phenomenal. It wasn't boo-hoo, it was heartstrings. . . . My feet were soaking from walking through the tears."[43]

Parsons and Richards became good friends and spent

considerable time together. During this period Richards and Rolling Stones lead singer Mick Jagger wrote several country rock hits influenced by Parsons, including "Honky Tonk Woman," "Dead Flowers," "Sweet Virginia," and "Wild Horses."

Cosmic American Music

In the early 1970s Gram Parsons released two well-received solo albums: *GP* and *Return of the Grievous Angel*. He was backed by members of Elvis Presley's band, many of whom had deep country roots. On several songs, Emmylou Harris, who Parsons discovered singing in a bar, provides soaring

The Flying Burrito Brothers pose in 1969 in their "Nudie" suits.

The Lasting Influence of Gram Parsons

During his lifetime, Gram Parsons was not successful, and his record sales were minimal. After he died in 1973, though, singer Emmylou Harris kept the Parsons legacy alive. She toured with his old band and popularized some of his songs, such as "Luxury Liner" and "Grievous Angel." In 1981 punk rocker Elvis Costello released an entire album of Parsons songs called *Almost Blue*. By the 1990s Parsons had become more popular in death than he was in life. In 1993 Rhino Records issued *Commemorativo: A Tribute to Gram Parsons*, with songs performed by alt-rockers such as the Mekons, Uncle Tupelo, and Peter Buck from R.E.M. In 1999 Harris produced the popular tribute album *Return of the Grievous Angel*, featuring Lucinda Williams, Steve Earle, Chrissie Hynde, Beck, and Sheryl Crow.

Parsons' daughter Polly has also been instrumental in popularizing her father's music. Between 1996 and 2006 she produced Gram Fest, also called the Cosmic American Music Festival, in Joshua Tree, California, where the singer died. In 2005 another Gram Parsons tribute concert, held in Santa Barbara, California, attracted Keith Richards, Norah Jones, Lucinda Williams, and other stars. Several books and films have been made about Parsons, and in 2008 Harris began efforts to have him inducted into the Country Music Hall of Fame in Nashville.

ethereal harmonies. Harris went on to become a star herself, mixing bluegrass, rock, honky-tonk, and swing styles during a career that lasted more than four decades.

Parsons was a rising star in 1973 when he overdosed on morphine and tequila just short of his twenty-seventh birthday. Long after his death, dozens of artists, including Elvis Costello, U2, Marty Stuart, Tom Petty, and the Eagles, credited Parsons for inspiring their music.

Despite his influence, Parsons felt contempt for country rock, the style of music he helped create. He believed the style lacked the authenticity and soul embodied by Merle Haggard, George Jones, and Hank Williams. Parsons made his feelings clear about country rock's biggest stars in a comment he made before his death: "The Eagles' music is bubblegum. It's got too much sugar in it. Life is tougher than they make it out to be."[44] Parsons preferred to call his sound "cosmic American music."[45]

Country Outlaws

After Gram Parsons died, an entire genre known as outlaw came to dominate country music throughout the 1970s. Keith Richards credits Parsons for paving the way for the outlaws: "Basically, you wouldn't have had Waylon Jennings, you wouldn't have had all of that outlaw movement without Gram Parsons. He showed them a new approach, that country music isn't just this narrow thing that appeals to rednecks. He did it single-handed."[46]

Country outlaws rebelled against the syrupy-sweet Nashville sound of the 1960s. Leading the way were Willie Nelson, left, and Waylon Jennings, seen here at the US Festival in 1983.

A Longhaired Redneck

David Allan Coe wrote some of the biggest hits of the outlaw era, including "Longhaired Redneck," "Willie, Waylon and Me," and "Take This Job and Shove It." According to veteran music journalist Peter Doggett, Coe was heralded as the wildest of the outlaws during a wild decade:

> David Allan Coe hailed from Akron, Ohio. . . . But in 1967 he drove into Nashville with a stash of songs and a trailer on which was painted "Mysterious Rhinestone Cowboy." [False stories] about this tattooed figure began to circulate throughout Music City—how he'd journeyed to Tennessee from Ohio State Prison, where he'd served time on death row. . . . He dressed like a biker, could handle a Harley-Davidson, and wore his long hair greased over his leather jacket—none of which annulled the fact that he was also a skilled songwriter. . . . David Allan Coe's career blossomed, and . . . Coe claimed [the outlaw] tag with pride: narrating his history in the third-person . . . he boasted, "The reason the term Outlaws came about was because David Allan Coe was a member of the Outlaws Motorcycle Club, and he got up on stage at a Waylon Jennings concert with his Outlaws colors on." . . . Coe's rock credibility was crushed when *Rolling Stone* investigated his criminal past and [was] unable to confirm [his stories]. They declared him a "rhinestone ripoff."

Peter Doggett. *Are You Ready For the Country.* New York: Penguin Books, 2001, pp. 367–368.

The leading outlaws—Jennings, Willie Nelson, David Allan Coe, and Bobby Bare—rebelled against the syrupy-sweet Nashville sound perfected in the 1960s. Rather than play songs picked by producers, the outlaws wrote their own material or picked songs they preferred. The outlaws also used their own road bands in the studio rather than play with session musicians who were not familiar with their repertoire. These bands had a hard-edged sound driven by loud pedal steels, twangy electric guitars, and the driving two-step country beat held down by a thumping bass.

The live-hard country sound of the outlaws appealed to both country and rock audiences. After Jennings recorded the Lee Clayton song "Ladies Love Outlaws" in 1972, released on an album of the same name, the movement took off. The renegade underground quickly became mainstream, and dozens of songs brandishing the outlaw attitude appeared on records. By 1976 the sound was so popular that *Wanted! The Outlaws* became the first country album to achieve platinum status, selling more than a million units.

A compilation of previously released songs by Jennings, Nelson, Tompall Glaser, and Jennings's wife Jessi Colter, *Wanted! The Outlaws* features classics such as "My Heroes Have Always Been Cowboys" and "Good-Hearted Woman." The songs were meant to appeal to both rock and country audiences. To sell the concept to rock fans, *Rolling Stone* editor Chet Flippo was asked to compose the liner notes for the album. Flippo wrote: "Progressive Country was on the map. And these are the people responsible for that. Call them outlaws, call them innovators, call them revolutionaries, call them what you will, they're just some damned fine people who are also some of the most gifted songwriters and singers anywhere."[47]

While artists such as Freddy Fender, Linda Hargrove, Mickey Newbury, Billy Joe Shaver, and Hank Williams Jr. rode the outlaw bandwagon, Jennings and Nelson sold the most records. Jennings had a huge hit singing about "Waylon and Willie and the boys" down in "Luckenbach, Texas." He also recorded duets in his rich baritone with Nelson that included "Mammas Don't Let Your Babies Grow Up to Be Cowboys." These songs quickly became staples of 1970s country—and even rock—radio. Meanwhile, Nelson's *Red Headed Stranger*—an album that shocked record executives for its sparse, acoustic arrangements—went platinum almost immediately upon its release.

Outlaw country dominated the charts with honest

songs about the lives of the performers. Rather than appeal to straitlaced country audiences, the outlaws sang "Wasted Days and Wasted Nights," "Whiskey Bent and Hell Bound," "Here I Am Drunk Again," and "Take This Job and Shove It."

Hot-Picking Hippies

As David Allan Coe's humorous "Longhaired Redneck" makes clear, most outlaws, despite appearances, remained true to Southern heritage and country roots. This could not be said for the long-haired hippies in California who introduced a new style of country to pop and rock audiences who had probably never heard of Roy Acuff or Ernest Tubb.

Commander Cody and His Lost Planet Airmen were among the first to play what Chet Flippo later called progressive country. Formed in Ann Arbor, Michigan, in 1967, the band migrated to San Francisco, California, where they recorded their first album, *Lost in the Ozone,* in 1971. Pianist George "Commander Cody" Frayne led an eight-piece group of virtuoso musicians who combined the sounds of Bob Wills' western swing with rockabilly, blues, and honky-tonk music. Commander Cody's group of hot-picking hippies singing about marijuana, alcohol, and truck driving gave original songs like "Wine Do Your Stuff," "Seeds and Stems (Again)," and "Lost in the Ozone" a level of irony and humor. Members of the Lost Planet Airmen showed off their numerous musical skills in the group's only top-ten hit, a remake of the 1950s rockabilly song "Hot Rod Lincoln."

While the San Francisco rock fans appreciated Commander Cody and His Lost Planet Airmen, country audiences did not. In 1973, when the group played at the Country & Western Convention in Nashville, they were booed off the stage as audience members yelled "get a haircut" and "find a rock concert."[48] By the mid-1970s the group's appeal to rock audiences also waned, and the Lost Planet Airmen broke up in 1977. In the twenty-first century, Frayne keeps the sound alive with the Commander Cody Band. He writes that he is "still trying to pound his piano into submission."[49]

Old and In The Way

Commander Cody often opened for the Grateful Dead, another counterculture group inspired by country music. Jerry Garcia, the renowned lead guitarist for the Dead, started his career at age fifteen playing the banjo. Like many others of his generation, Garcia, who was born in 1942, listened to the *Grand Ole Opry* on the radio every Saturday night. In the early 1960s Garcia played bluegrass music in San Francisco coffeehouses and bars.

Garcia formed the Grateful Dead in 1965, and within a few years they were known as masters of West Coast psychedelic rock, playing twenty-five-minute jams filled with rolling drum solos, feedback, and screaming lead guitar. Garcia never forgot his roots and remained intensely interested in bluegrass music. In his words, it was "an itch I'd had for a long time."[50]

In 1973 Garcia decided to scratch that itch with Old and In The Way, a band he formed with a group of bluegrass musicians. Besides Garcia, the group consisted of mandolin player Dave Grisman, bassist John Kahn, and guitarist Peter Rowan, a former member of Bill Monroe's Bluegrass Boys. The group's fiddle player, Vassar Clements, had recently achieved national recognition for his work on the popular bluegrass revival album *Will the Circle Be Unbroken*, featuring Earl Scruggs, Doc Watson, and the Nitty Gritty Dirt Band.

Old and In The Way played classic bluegrass tunes, such as Monroe's "Uncle Pen," along with originals by Grisman, Rowan, and Clements. Because of his commitment to the Grateful Dead, Garcia could not maintain his leading role in the band. By the time the eponymous album *Old and In The Way* was released in 1975, the group had disbanded.

Despite its short life, Old and In The Way introduced bluegrass to a counterculture audience raised on the Beatles, the Dead, and the Rolling Stones. Bob Dylan was also a fan, and in his typical, cryptic roundabout way, he described Garcia's playing as "the very spirit personified of whatever is muddy river country at its core and screams up into the spheres."[51]

Will the Circle Be Unbroken

In 1972 the California-based Nitty Gritty Dirt Band brought together an all-star lineup of old-time bluegrass musicians for the triple album *Will the Circle Be Unbroken*. The album included venerable Grand Ole Opry stars such as "Mother" Maybelle Carter, Merle Travis, Earl Scruggs, and Jimmy Martin. Other players, such as Doc Watson, Norman Blake, and Vassar Clements, were virtually unknown outside bluegrass circles. Most participants in the project had been forgotten in the early 1970s when countrypolitan was the main sound issued by Nashville.

Will the Circle Be Unbroken is filled with hot picking, singing, and vocal harmony. Every track was recorded live, and most of the songs on the album are either first or second takes. Without a single sour note or missed lick, the album's raw, rolling bluegrass sound was a hit among a new generation unfamiliar with the Opry or its classic stars. As AllMusic editor Bruce Elder writes, "This was the first real country album that a lot of rock listeners under the age of 30 ever heard. Thus, it opened up pathways and dialogue in all directions, across several generations and cultural barriers."

Bruce Elder. "Will the Circle Be Unbroken." AllMusic (2011), www.allmusic.com/album/will-the-circle-be-unbroken-r67595.

Back to the Middle

The progressive bluegrass, hippie honky-tonk, and outlaw sounds made their mark on country music, but also created a backlash in Nashville. Even as the progressive movement was in full swing, there was a concerted effort among the country music establishment to promote the traditional Nashville sound. This was typified in one of the decade's biggest hits, Glen Campbell's 1975 "Rhinestone Cowboy," recorded with a soaring countrypolitan string section. With its sentimental lyrics about a battered country singer hoping one day to shine like a rhinestone cowboy, the song rose to number one on both the country and pop charts.

Kenny Rogers was one of the most prominent rhinestone-studded country hit makers in the late 1970s. Rogers topped pop and country charts with 1977's "Lucille," a sentimental song about a woman who left her man with "four

A backlash to more progressive country music by the Nashville establishment pushed Glen Campbell's "Rhinestone Cowboy" to number one on the country and pop charts in 1975.

hungry children and a crop in the field." Rogers achieved superstar status the following year with "The Gambler." Following this success, Rogers teamed up with Dottie West to record several albums of syrupy pop duets that were pure countrypolitan.

By 1980 a new category of music, defined by commercial radio programmers, was growing in popularity. Known as middle-of-the-road, or MOR, this musical format was meant to appeal to the largest audience while avoiding sounds that were loud, edgy, or experimental. Stars like Rogers and Campbell specifically tailored their music for country and MOR radio, and they succeeded brilliantly. By the early 1980s the outlaw movement was pronounced dead by the Nashville establishment. It would take a younger collection of musicians to return country to it roots and leave the middle of the road in the rearview mirror.

CHAPTER 6

Old and New Traditions

By the early 1980s Nashville, Tennessee, record companies were committed to the formulaic countrypolitan sound that had brought them great success. During this era, squeaky-clean artists such as Debbie Boone, Tanya Tucker, Ronnie Milsap, Lee Greenwood, and Janie Fricke were performing middle-of-the-road pop songs marketed as country music. With raw, outlaw country falling off the charts, tunes such as Boone's excessively sentimental "You Light Up My Life" and Johnny Lee's overproduced "Lookin' for Love" were an unabashed return to the Music City sound of the 1960s. As the countrypolitan stars sold millions of records, music critic Boris Weintraub of the *Washington Star* wrote, "Perhaps it is time to find a new term to replace 'country.' Because good or bad, there is precious little country left in today's country music."[52]

Urban Cowboys

Boris Weintraub's comment came at the beginning of what was called the urban cowboy era. The term was derived from a 1978 article in *Esquire* that described oil workers who spent their nights at a huge honky-tonk in Pasadena, Texas, called Gilley's, owned by outlaw singer Mickey Gilley. The men at Gilley's dressed like cowboys, drank numerous beers,

Urban Cowboy

Country music made it to the silver screen in the 1980s, as movies such as Willie Nelson's *Honeysuckle Rose*, Dolly Parton's *Nine to Five*, and Loretta Lynn's *Coal Miner's Daughter* introduced mainstream America to the lives of country hit makers. But it was the movie *Urban Cowboy* that did the most to make the country music culture a national fad. The film featured then Hollywood sex symbol John Travolta, playing Bud, a young farmer who moves to Houston to work on the oil rigs. Travolta had starred in the disco dance hit *Saturday Night Fever* only two years earlier. When Travolta traded his white disco suit for jeans and a cowboy hat, *Urban Cowboy* became the country version of *Saturday Night Fever.*

Urban Cowboy featured line dancing, mechanical bulls, and country fashions. These fads quickly spread across the United States as country bars reminiscent of Gilley's, the honky-tonk featured in the film, opened everywhere from Los Angeles to Akron, Ohio, and New York City. Country record sales also jumped, moving from about 10 percent of the market in the late 1970s to 15 percent in 1982.

and took turns riding a mechanical bull. The article inspired the 1980 movie *Urban Cowboy,* starring John Travolta and Debra Winger. *Urban Cowboy* was one of the top-grossing films of the era, and the sound track, with songs by Gilley, Johnny Lee, the Eagles, Kenny Rogers, and other country acts, produced two multiplatinum albums.

Urban Cowboy kicked off a fad for cowboy boots, Stetson hats, designer blue jeans, and pickup trucks. In response, thousands of bars across the country installed mechanical bulls and hosted nights dedicated to a two-step country line dance called the Cotton Eyed Joe. Like all trends, the urban cowboy fad peaked quickly and crashed just as fast. Casual fans attracted to country and western moved on, and by 1985 there was a drastic decrease in country music sales.

Alabama Puts the Country Back in Country

After the urban cowboy sensation, things looked bleak for the countrypolitan sound on Nashville's Music Row. One of the few bright spots came from a group of talented musicians who grew up around the cotton fields of Fort Payne, Alabama. Guitarist Randy Owen, bassist Teddy Gentry, and keyboard and fiddle player Jeff Cook were cousins. They formed the appropriately named group Alabama with drummer Mark Herndon in 1977. Raised on traditional honky-tonk, hard country, and country rock, Alabama was determined to put the traditional country sounds of bluegrass and honky-tonk back into country music.

The band Alabama is among the top selling acts in music history, with thirty number-one records and more than 73 million records sold.

Alabama had its first hit with "Tennessee River" the year *Urban Cowboy* was released. The song has the driving two-step beat, tight three-part harmonies, a distorted rock guitar, and an anthem-like sing-along chorus. The song breaks

into a lightning-fast fiddle breakdown in the middle. This musical formula was put to work on Alabama's subsequent releases. This sound appealed to both traditional country music fans and younger folks raised on rock. As Kurt Wolff writes: "Gently blending pop and country into easily digestible formulas, their sound appeals across generations; they're just rebellious enough for the young folks, but their parents also dig the boys' pretty harmonies, sentimental soft spots, and old-fashioned family values."[53]

Everything Alabama recorded turned to gold. The group racked up twenty-one number-one records between 1980 and 1987. In 1989 Alabama was elected Artist of the Decade by the Academy of Country Music (ACM). By the time Herndon quit in 2007, the band had scored thirty number-one hits and sold more than 73 million records. Those sales figures place Alabama among the top-selling acts in music history, a list that includes Elvis Presley, the Beatles, and the Rolling Stones.

Alabama was one of the first bands to gain acceptance in a business that generally promoted individual singers. The group's popularity showed producers that youth-oriented country bands could sell records, and a host of groups such as Sawyer Brown, Southern Pacific, the Desert Rose Band, and the Kentucky Headhunters were promoted throughout the 1980s.

The Judds Turn It Loose

Like Alabama, the Judds were a family act that reaped great rewards appealing to a multigenerational audience during the 1980s. The singing mother-daughter group from Kentucky combined mother Naomi's traditional country roots with daughter Wynonna's modern sensibilities. Naomi was thirty-six and Wynonna was only eighteen years old in 1982 when the Judds were signed by RCA.

In 1984 the Judds released "Mama He's Crazy," a breakout hit single that peaked at number one and won the Judds a Grammy for Best Country Vocal by a Duo or Group. With its simple production, acoustic guitar, and dominant pedal steel, the song has an old-time honky-tonk feel. During the next five years, the Judds were unstoppable, recording thirteen more chart toppers in a row. The music was a blend of traditional country, blues, rock, bluegrass, and pop and helped make the Judds one of the most successful duos in country music history.

Judds songs such as the swinging, stomping "Girls Night Out" present Wynonna as an assertive, strong country woman. This appealing image is also present on "Turn It Loose" and "I Know Where I'm Going," hits that helped popularize country music to a new group of young female fans.

Due to ill health, Naomi retired in 1991. Wynonna launched a solo career the following year. Her first album, *Wynonna*, was an immediate smash hit, selling more than 3 million copies. Her next album, *Tell Me Why*, achieved similar success. In 1993 Wynonna published her best-selling autobiography, *Love Can Build a Bridge*, which was later turned into a TV movie.

Since 2001, Wynonna and Naomi have held periodic musical reunions, which produce sold-out concerts and top-selling songs. In 2009 Wynonna continued her musical journey with *Sing Chapter 1*, an album of vintage pop, country, and swing songs that showcase the bluesy voice that drove the Judds' sound for a quarter century.

The music of the Judds was part of a new style that developed in the early 1980s and came to dominate country music in the following years. Known as neotraditional, new traditional, or simply new country, the genre was a reaction to the overproduced, slick country music that was emanating from Music Row during the *Urban Cowboy* era. And the biggest stars of new country were not based in Nashville but in Texas, Oklahoma, and even California. These neotraditionalists fueled the biggest commercial boom in country music history.

George Strait's New Traditions

George Strait is one of the founding fathers of the neotraditional movement. Born in 1952, Strait grew up on a huge Texas cattle ranch. He formed a country band, Ace in

the Hole, in 1975. Strait's music was strongly influenced by the western swing of Bob Wills, the hard-core honky-tonk traditions of Hank Williams, the barroom ballads of Lefty Frizzell, and the Bakersfield sound of Merle Haggard.

Strait released his first single, "Unwound," in 1981 and followed with the album *Strait Country.* Both quickly reached number one. According to music journalist David Dicaire, "Strait's record drew deeply from the honky-tonk tradition, bypassing the trappings of lush country-pop crossovers, Outlaw and Urban Cowboy swagger and country-rock; it pointed the genre to a new future direction."[54]

Strait's success reached historical proportions with a string of down-home country hits. Throughout the 1980s, every one of Strait's albums contained at least one number-one single and reached gold status, selling more than five hundred thousand copies, or achieved platinum sales. By 2011 Strait had sold nearly 69 million albums and accumulated fifty-eight number-one singles, breaking a record for solo country music artists previously held by Conway Twitty. Strait was also nominated for more Country Music

George Strait, performing in concert in 1983, holds the record for most number one country singles by a solo artist as of 2011.

Association and Academy of Country Music awards than any other artist.

Hunks in Hats

George Strait has been cited as an influence by Alan Jackson and Garth Brooks, two members of what is known as the Class of '89. Jackson and Brooks were part of a group of country superstars, including Clint Black, Dwight Yoakam, and Travis Tritt, who all had their first hits in 1989. These singers had roots in neotraditionalism, but infused their music with a youthful sound and a rock-and-roll feel.

Like Strait, the Class of '89 valued musical virtuosity and honesty. The neotraditionalists looked to the elders of country music for their inspiration. Their sounds relied on rich Southern-accented vocals sung over driving rock drumbeats, hot-picking electric guitars, and screaming fiddles. Orchestrated string sections and syrupy backup vocals were banished.

While the Class of '89 based their sound on musical honesty, their image was pure entertainment. With the growing popularity of Country Music Television in the early '90s, the music videos produced by the new country artists featured what Kurt Wolff describes as "hunks in hats, pretty gals in boots, and bright-eyed freshly scrubbed faces."[55]

While some in Nashville balked at new country's flash, few could argue with its astonishing financial success. Driven by the growing popularity of music videos, country album sales doubled from $500 million to $1 billion between 1989 and 1991. They doubled again by 1995, and by 1996 two out of every three albums on the country charts achieved gold, platinum, or multiplatinum status.

Garth Brooks Rocks

Oklahoma-born Garth Brooks was at the head of country music's economic boom time. His 1991 album *Ropin' the Wind* debuted at number one on the pop and country charts—the first country album to ever do so—and eventually sold more than 10 million copies. Brooks was more than a record executive's dream. With his down-home personality, he put his family first and, like George Strait, represented the humble and endearing values of country music.

When he strapped on his guitar and took to the stage, however, Brooks took his cues more from rocker Bruce Springsteen than from honky-tonker Hank Williams. He jumped, danced, strutted, swung from the rafters on cables, and occasionally smashed his guitar, all the while singing into his headset microphone. This brand of hard-rocking country appealed to a huge audience of urban, suburban, and country fans.

Garth Brooks' hard-rocking country style appeals to a large audience of urban, suburban, and country fans.

Country Line Dancing

People have been dancing to the fiddles, guitars, and mandolins of country music for centuries. In many rural regions, the Saturday-night square dance at a local barn was one of the few sources of entertainment. Line dancing, which originated in the 1700s, was also popular. Line dancing involves a large group of people arranged in a line facing the same direction, executing coordinated dance steps.

In 1992 the popularity of line dancing reached dizzying heights thanks to country singer Billy Ray Cyrus. His song "Achy Breaky Heart," with its driving two-step beat, peaked on both country and pop charts. The video, shown in heavy rotation on CMT, shows a large group of people line dancing and helped make the dance style a national craze. Around the same time, the country music duo Brooks & Dunn released "Boot Scootin' Boogie," a tribute to the Texas honky-tonk line dancing style. In the years that followed, country dance halls filled with line dancers dressed in tight jeans, cowboy boots, and western shirts and hats. By the end of the 1990s thousands of country line dancing clubs proliferated in the United States, and dancers could learn steps from countless instructional videos and dance classes.

By drawing crowds more associated with rock music festivals, and by selling more than 66 million albums throughout the 1990s, Brooks changed the country music industry. For example, Brooks attracted more than two hundred thousand people to New York City's Central Park for a free concert in 1997, and by the end of the 1990s he was selling out stadiums in a matter of minutes. This success created a demand for other country acts such as Clint Black, Alan Jackson, and Vince Gill, who all had their roots in neotraditionalism but whose beat was closer to country rock.

Twain Comes on Over

Shania Twain was perhaps the most controversial of the new country artists, at least when she first arrived on the scene in 1993. Born in Ontario, Canada, Twain starred in videos featuring lively dance routines and provocative outfits. She seemed to be mimicking the pop star Madonna.

Twain projected a telegenic image, but it was her music that endeared her to country music fans raised on rock and roll and music video television. Her producer and then-husband, Robert John "Mutt" Lange, previously worked with heavy metal bands such as Def Leppard and AC/DC. Lange's rock-and-roll roots can be heard in Twain's unique sound, which blends new country, pop, honky-tonk, rockabilly, and swing.

Twain's first two albums, *The Woman in Me* and *Come on Over,* sold an astounding 10 million copies each. This made Twain the first female artist to sell 10 million albums back-to-back. Not everyone loved Twain, though, as AllMusic editor Stephen Thomas Erlewine explains: "[Critics] accused her of diluting country with bland, anthemic hard rock techniques and shamelessly selling her records with sexy videos. Fans ignored such complaints, mainly because her audience was comprised of many listeners who had grown accustomed to such marketing strategies by constant exposure to MTV."[56]

Women in the New Tradition

Shania Twain and the Judds were among an increasingly influential group of female artists, including k.d. lang and Nanci Griffith, who were playing the neotraditional style. Griffith, a singer-songwriter from Texas, was discovered by Nashville producers playing folk music in Austin, Texas. Griffith infused her country music with the understated acoustic sounds of folk, a sound she dubbed folkabilly. Griffith lived in Nashville for a short time in 1985, where she wrote songs for other artists. One Griffith song, "Love at the Five and Dime," was a hit for country artist Kathy Mattea in 1986, while "Outbound Plane" was a chart topper for Suzy Bogguss in 1991. Despite her success, Griffith was unhappy with the Nashville music establishment and preferred to record her own brand of critically acclaimed folkabilly without the input of Music City veterans.

Two other women who played the new traditional style,

The Kookiest Traditionalist

Of all the neotraditionalist singers, k.d. lang may be the most distinctive. A true Nashville outsider, born in Canada, lang is undoubtedly one of the only vegetarian lesbians to top the country music charts. In the late 1980s lang's amazingly rich, textured voice and authentic 1940s and 1950s country sound attracted widespread attention. Her 1988 album Shadowland *and 1989 album* Absolute Torch and Twang *were both awarded gold records. The albums held a unique status, topping both the mainstream country charts and the alternative underground charts occupied by alt-rock groups like R.E.M. and Sonic Youth. Robert Oermann describes lang's style:*

Easily the kookiest of [the new traditionalists], lang had a wildly physical stage show, wore a spikey crew-cut hairdo, and dressed in

"retro" square-dance skirts, embroidered cowgirl blouses, and cut-off western boots. But she also had a wallop of a voice and devoutly wished to be a reincarnation of Patsy Cline. Fans as well as Nashville insiders loved her over-the-top performances, but radio shunned her records.

Robert K. Oermann. *A Century of Country.* New York: TV Books, 1999, p. 294.

k.d. lang's unique style and rich, textured voice helped her albums top the country and alternative charts.

Carlene Carter and Rosanne Cash, are stepsisters who both grew up in Nashville. They are referred to as country royalty because of their musical family heritage. Carlene Carter is the daughter of 1950s honky-tonk star Carl Smith and June Carter Cash, who herself is the daughter of Maybelle Carter of the pioneering country music group the Carter Family. Rosanne Cash is the child of Johnny Cash and his first wife,

Vivian. (June Carter married Johnny Cash in 1965 after the girls were born.)

Carlene Carter mixed a contagious blend of country, rock, swing, rockabilly, and honky-tonk on her 1990 breakthrough album *I Fell in Love.* Her sound was achieved with a cast of country and rock luminaries that included guitarist James Burton, who backed Elvis Presley; drummer Jim Keltner, who played with John Lennon after the Beatles broke up; and backup singer Nicolette Larson, who sang with Neil Young as well as recording her own best-selling album.

Rosanne Cash also experimented with various styles, playing traditional country on the album *Seven Year Ache,* then shocking Nashville—and many of her fans—by recording the new wave–tinged *Rhythm and Romance.* As the daughter of Johnny Cash, she was able to follow her own musical instincts in a city bound by tradition. In doing so, Rosanne Cash managed to top the country charts eleven times in the 1980s.

Reba's Kind of Country

Reba McEntire was another artist who rejected the Nashville sound to achieve success. Born in Oklahoma, McEntire grew up riding at rodeo events. She moved to Nashville in 1974, but achieved only minor success for a decade. McEntire finally became a major star when she embraced neotraditionalism in 1984. The record *My Kind of Country* was McEntire's sixth album, but the first one on which she asserts her own identity, ironically, while covering old honky-tonk favorites by Ray Price, Faron Young, and Connie Smith. McEntire's traditional arrangements and expressive voice, which convey sorrow, anger, and joy, helped her find common cause with the neotraditionalists.

In 1984 McEntire won the prestigious Female Vocalist of the Year award from the CMA, beating superstars such as Dolly Parton and Barbara Mandrell. By the end of the 1980s, McEntire's brand of neotraditionalism made her one of the top-selling acts of the era, and her success rolled on for decades. Today she is recognized as a country music

Reba McEntire's brand of neotraditionalism made her one of the top selling acts of the 1980s.

icon whose gold, platinum, and multiplatinum records helped make her the dominant female voice of the new country era.

The Dixie Chicks

The sounds of new traditionalism were firmly established by the late 1980s when sisters Martie and Emily Erwin joined forces to form the Dixie Chicks. Martie was a fiddle player who finished third in the National Fiddle Championship in 1989, while Emily was a virtuoso on banjo, guitar, Dobro, accordion, and bass. The first incarnation of the band included Laura Lynch on upright bass and guitarist Robin Lynn Macy.

The Dixie Chicks built a following playing at bluegrass festivals and opening for major acts such as Garth Brooks, Reba McEntire, and George Strait. In 1992 Natalie Maines joined the group as lead singer after Lynch and Macy dropped out. As a trio, the Dixie Chicks utilized the old-time bluegrass sound of fiddle, banjo, and guitar. The group maintained a minor level of success until 1998, when their album *Wide Open Spaces* quickly sold 6 million copies, making it the biggest-selling album ever by a country group. Sales were boosted by the band's clever videos, in heavy rotation on CMT, which featured the attractive young women showing off their musical skills while clowning around in airports, on tour buses, and onstage.

The Dixie Chicks's sound has been described as neo, or new, bluegrass, popular with both country and pop audiences. In a business geared toward a conservative, middle-aged audience, the Dixie Chicks were notable because about 60 percent of their records sold to people younger than twenty-five. Maines damaged the band's reputation among traditional country fans, however, when on March 10, 2003—just nine days before the United States invaded Iraq—she criticized President George W. Bush, a fellow Texan. From the stage at a small club in London, England, she exclaimed: "Just so you know, we're on the good side with y'all. We do not want this war, this violence, and we're ashamed that the president of the United States is from Texas."[57]

An uproar followed after Maines's statement was publicized in the American media. The Dixie Chicks received hundreds of death threats, their songs were banned from country radio, and the group was loudly booed at concerts that followed. In several cities, Dixie Chicks CDs were burned or crushed by bulldozers at public events sponsored by talk radio disc jockeys.

Although Maines apologized, the Dixie Chicks never returned to their previous popularity. Maines forgot that even if Shania Twain was showing her navel and Reba McEntire was subtly promoting feminist values, most country fans continued to value the conservative tradition in the neotraditional sound.

CHAPTER 7

Alt, Progressive, and Pop Country

I n October 2001 in San Francisco, California, thousands of people gathered for a free concert called the Strictly Bluegrass Festival in Golden Gate Park. With people throwing Frisbees, sitting on blankets, and dancing in the sun, the scene was reminiscent of the 1960s when as many as fifty thousand people came to the park to hear free shows by the Grateful Dead and Jefferson Airplane. But instead of blasting electric guitars, throbbing basses, and exploding drums, there were acoustic guitars, mandolins, fiddles, pedal steel guitars, and stand-up basses. The first Strictly Bluegrass Festival featured Emmylou Harris, Alison Krauss, and a few other bluegrass acts.

The Strictly Bluegrass Festival was the brainchild of Warren Hellman, a billionaire venture capitalist, banjo player, and bluegrass enthusiast. The first concert was a huge success. By 2002 the concert had grown to two days and the roster of acts increased to include Harris, Peter Rowan, and a wide array of progressive bluegrass acts with names like Belle Monroe & Her Brewglass Boys and Strung Over.

In 2003 Hellman felt the term *strictly bluegrass* limited the scope of the festival, so he added the word *hardly* to the name and added a third day of festivities. In the following years the Hardly Strictly Bluegrass (HSB) festival became a showcase for twenty-first-century country music. The lineup featured

Neko Case

With her searing vocals and quirky songs, Neko Case's music and songwriting blends the best of Loretta Lynn, Hank Williams, and even Bob Dylan. In doing so she delivers toe-tapping mediations, dark alt-country despair, and blue midnight moods. Case was born in Alexandria, Virginia, in 1970, and launched a cross-border career in 1994 that spanned Tacoma and Seattle, Washington, and Vancouver, Canada. Her highly acclaimed 1997 debut album, *The Virginian*, has a smoky, reverb-drenched 1950s feel, with Case covering songs by Lynn and Ernest Tubb.

Case's next two albums, *Furnace Room Lullaby* (2000) and *Blacklisted* (2002), contain material she wrote or cowrote. On these records, Case's echoing, minor-key songs are cinematic, invoking images from old cowboy movies. The albums earned widespread accolades from critics and fans alike.

Case became a favorite on late-night talk shows like *Late Night with Jimmy Fallon*, and the publicity helped her 2009 album, *Middle Cyclone*, reach number three on the *Billboard* charts. It was her first album to crack the top ten. Critics agree that Case could have easily been a huge country pop star if she so chose. However, she remained true to her eclectic vision and produced honest music with a dark atmosphere so thick it could be cut with a knife.

respected veterans like Merle Haggard and Earl Scruggs alongside a wide array of younger country acts such as Southern Culture on the Skids, Neko Case, Béla Fleck, and Gillian Welch, and Alison Krauss. The free festival also attracted a growing legion of fans, with more than six hundred thousand music lovers attending the three-day event in 2011.

The Bluegrass Revival

Many of the stars who appeared at Hardly Strictly Bluegrass are known as progressive bluegrass musicians. Their fresh

Alison Krauss performs with Robert Plant at the 2008 Austin City Limits music festival. Their critically acclaimed album Raising Sand *won the Grammy for Album of the year in 2009.*

sounds contributed to a twenty-first-century bluegrass revival. Rather than rehashing the music of Bill Monroe and Earl Scruggs, progressive bluegrass players added new chord changes, tempos, and attitudes to a beloved old-timey style.

One of the leading artists of the bluegrass revival, Alison Krauss, was born in 1971 and grew up in Decatur, Illinois. She won her first national fiddle contest at the age of thirteen. Two years later, Krauss was signed to a recording contract. In addition to her great fiddle playing, Krauss has a high soprano voice that David Dicaire describes as "truly angelic . . . her vocal range is suited to the material she often sings, which is about lost love."[58]

Throughout the early 1990s Krauss alternated between recording with her band Union Station and making solo albums. In 1995 she attained a level of success no traditional bluegrass act had ever accomplished. Her album *Now That I've Found You: A Collection* went double platinum and she won four CMA awards, including Best Single, Best Female

O Brother, Where Art Thou?

As the creators of country pop generated billions of dollars in the early twenty-first century, some in the industry forgot that country fans love tradition. As a result of this oversight, country radio stations at first refused to play songs from *O Brother, Where Art Thou?*, the 2000 soundtrack album from the film of the same name. *O Brother* features old-time string-band songs that were popular in the 1930s, before the style evolved into bluegrass. The album includes the original "Big Rock Candy Mountain" by "Haywire Mac" McClintock along with remakes of "I'll Fly Away" by Alison Krauss and Gillian Welch and "Keep On the Sunny Side" by the family vocal group the Whites.

After the film *O Brother, Where Art Thou?* was released, the CD quickly sold a million copies. By April 2001 thousands of fans were calling and e-mailing radio stations to request Dan Tyminski and Union Station's version of "Man of Constant Sorrow." This helped *O Brother* gain new fans, and in 2002 the album was at the top of the country charts for five months. *O Brother, Where Art Thou?* eventually sold more than 8 million copies, won five Grammys, and spurred renewed interest in string-band music. In 2010 the NPR program *All Songs Considered* named the album one of "The Decade's 50 Most Important Recordings."

Vocalist, and Best Emerging Artist. Krauss also won two Grammys.

Krauss's success continued well into the twenty-first century. In 2000 she expanded her fan base with her three-song contribution to the multiplatinum soundtrack for the movie *O Brother, Where Art Thou?* In 2004 her album with Union Station, *Lonely Runs Both Ways,* achieved double platinum status driven by two number-one hits, "Restless" and "If I Didn't Know Any Better." In 2007 Krauss strengthened her alt-country credentials recording the album *Raising Sand* with Robert Plant, best known as the wailing lead singer of the 1970s hard-rock supergroup Led Zeppelin.

Raising Sand met with extensive critical acclaim and won the 2009 Grammy for Album of the Year. By this time, Krauss had won more Grammy awards than any other female artist in history. She did so by giving old sounds a fresh new take.

This helped promote the bluegrass revival and popularize the good old sound of fiddles, mandolins, and Dobros in a new century.

Alternative Country

Alternative country, or alt-country, was another popular new sound at the Hardly Strictly Bluegrass festival. *Alt-country* is a term used for artists who combine a wide variety of sounds that might include honky-tonk, rock, blues, punk, and other musical elements. The sound is lively, edgy, and rarely heard on country radio. Alt-country singers often have a less-polished vocal sound, and their raw musical arrangements give the feeling of a live performance. While the definition of alt-country is sometimes hard to pin down, popular artists working in the genre, including Wilco, Neko Case, Southern Culture on the Skids, and Iron & Wine, all cultivate original music that sets them apart from the biggest hit makers in modern country pop.

A fine example of the alt-country sound may be heard on the 1998 Grammy-winning album *Car Wheels on a Gravel Road* by Lucinda Williams, who was referred to by *Spin* magazine as the "lovestruck alt-country queen."[59] Williams delayed the release of the album for several years. She had a problem with the overproduced Nashville sound of her vocals. After a long battle with her record company, Williams moved production to California, where she was able to achieve the sound she desired. AllMusic reviewer Steve Huey explains: "The production . . . throws Williams' idiosyncratic voice into sharp relief, to the point where it's noticeably separate from the band. As a result, every inflection and slight tonal alteration is captured."[60]

Beyond nurturing production value, Williams writes mesmerizing lyrics that explore uncomfortable topics rarely covered in modern country music. The song "Drunken Angel," for example, is about a talented but derelict musician who is shot and killed in a senseless argument. "Concrete and Barbed Wire" is written from the viewpoint of a woman whose boyfriend is in prison. "Greenville" details a woman's heartbreaking relationship with an abusive, drunken musician.

There is no denying Lucinda Williams has created a unique sound that could not be confused with any other artist. After the success of *Car Wheels on a Gravel Road,* Williams pursued an even more stripped-down sound. Her 2001 follow-up album, *Essence,* is filled with laid-back songs that, for the most part, highlight Williams' voice and acoustic guitar. The bluesy songs on 2003's *World Without Tears* feature teary lyrics, slow-tempo songs, and spare arrangements.

The Old-Fashioned Outlaw Toby Keith

While alt-country and progressive bluegrass helped expand the country music audience in the 2000s, the best-selling artists of the decade had roots in the neotraditionalist movement of the 1990s. Toby Keith started his career in 1993 as a contemporary of new country artists Garth Brooks and Alan Jackson. As a young man growing up in Clinton, Oklahoma, in the 1970s, he was inspired by Bob Wills and Merle Haggard.

Keith produced several platinum albums in the late 1990s, but his fame exploded when he expressed his political beliefs in 2002. Keith wrote the song "Courtesy of the Red, White and Blue (The Angry American)" as a response to the terrorist attacks of September 11, 2001. The revenge song is about waving the flag, the Statue of Liberty shaking her fist in anger, and dropping bombs on terrorists. One line informs terrorists that putting a boot in their rear end is the American way. This stirred up widespread controversy, and made Keith a household name. Hard-core country fans propelled the single to number one, and it also crossed over to the Top 25 pop charts.

Keith followed his successful single in 2003 with *Shock'n Y'all.* The album contains the patriotic tributes "American Soldier" and "The Taliban Song." The politics are tempered by hard-drinking honky-tonk anthems like "I Love This Bar" and "Whiskey Girl." Although Keith gained attention for his angry songs, politics are not his main concern, as Stephen Thomas Erlewine explains:

Since Toby Keith not only can come across as a loud-mouth redneck but seems to *enjoy* being a loudmouth redneck, it's easy for some listeners to dismiss him as a backwoods right-wing crank. . . . Those listeners aren't entirely wrong, since he can succumb to reactionary politics . . . but Keith isn't coming from a [moralistic] right-wing standpoint. He's an old-fashioned, cantankerous outlaw who's eager to be as oversized and larger than life as legends like Waylon Jennings, Merle

Toby Keith's strong political beliefs and patriotic lyrics helped propel him to superstar status.

Haggard and Willie Nelson, who bucked conventions and spoke their minds.[61]

Whatever Keith's motivations, his rough-and-rowdy sounds continued to top the country music charts every year throughout the 2000s and into the 2010s. Keith's fifteenth studio album, 2011's *Clancy's Tavern*, featured the number-one single "Made In America," about an old farming couple who will only buy products made in the United States. A second song from the album, "Red Solo Cup," balances out the political statement with another drinking song. The video, about red cups used at beer keg parties, went viral on the video-sharing website YouTube, receiving six hundred thousand hits within days of posting.

Keith makes a point of backing his political words with patriotic actions. Between 2005 and 2011, the superstar country singer participated in nine weeklong USO tours where he entertained American troops in Iraq, Afghanistan, and at sea on aircraft carriers. Unlike some USO entertainers who only play on large bases, Keith insists on playing at forward-operating bases in the middle of dangerous war zones. Commenting on his dedication to American soldiers, Keith stated: "Since my first tour, I've been hooked on performing for troops. I start looking forward to my next USO trip the minute I touch down here in the States. I love it and I love our troops, they are the best in the world."[62]

Coasting with Kenny Chesney

Kenny Chesney, like Toby Keith, had fifteen albums under his belt by 2011, and produced top-ten hits every year. While Keith's style stuck close to his neotraditional honky-tonk roots, Chesney's music changed over time. While he started out in 1995 with a neotraditional and hard-country style, Chesney spent the following years sailing his yacht in the Caribbean and living in the Virgin Islands, where he heard the reggae and calypso music that inspired him to infuse his style with Caribbean sounds, making it unique on country radio.

Chesney's first move in a new direction can be heard on the 2002 pop-crossover hit single "On the Coast of Somewhere

Beautiful," from the album *No Shoes, No Shirt, No Problems.* The record, with its drifting sailboat feel, established a new direction for Chesney. His follow-up album, *When the Sun Goes Down*, was saturated with laid-back island music in a style perfected by pop star Jimmy Buffett in the 1980s.

Chesney remained true to his country roots as he continued to blend radio-friendly country with songs about beach bums, palm trees, and tropical islands. The 2005 album *Be As You Are* is a good example of this mix, with slow sentimental country pop songs like "Old Blue Chair" next to island calypso rockers like "Guitars and Tiki Bars." In 2008 Chesney combined country, rock, and reggae beats in "Everybody Wants to Go to Heaven."

Chesney's record-setting concert tours are among the most popular in the country music industry. His 2007 Flip-Flop Summer Tour was the highest-grossing country tour of the year, and his performances earned him CMA Entertainer of the Year awards in 2004, 2006, 2007, and 2008.

Taylor Swift Is Fearless

Kenny Chesney was among a group of male country music veterans, including Brad Paisley and Keith Urban, who dominated the charts in the mid-2000s. While these older, experienced musicians played for mature fans, one of their biggest competitors, Taylor Swift, was a young woman barely out of high school. Swift's amazing talent for writing songs about mean boys, stolen kisses, and wedding whims appealed to teenage girls. This coveted audience bought a lot of Swift's CDs, attended many concerts, and purchased mountains of T-shirts and other merchandise.

Swift was born in 1989, the same year Garth Brooks and Alan Jackson released their first albums. A native of Pennsylvania, Swift was only eleven when she traveled to Nashville with dreams of obtaining a major record deal. Although she visited every company on Music Row with a

Taylor Swift performs at Madison Square Garden in New York City in 2009. She has a coveted teenage girl fan base with crossover appeal into the pop music market.

demo tape, Swift returned home unsuccessful. In order to help her pursue her career, Swift's family moved to Nashville. Her luck soon improved. In 2003 the now fourteen-year-old Swift's songwriting talents impressed executives at Sony/ATV. She was hired as a staff songwriter, making her the youngest person to ever have that job.

When not working, Swift performed at the Bluebird Cafe, a Nashville songwriter's showcase. She was spotted by a talent scout for the newly formed label Big Machine Records and was signed to a recording contract in 2005. The following year, at the age of sixteen, Swift released her first single, "Tim McGraw," a wistful song about a lost summer love. The music video, which shows Swift romping in a field with a handsome boy, catapulted the beautiful young country singer to instant stardom and became a staple on CMT.

Swift's debut smash single was soon followed by the album *Taylor Swift*, which quickly peaked at number one on the *Billboard* Top Country Album charts and crossed over to achieve number five on the *Billboard* 200 pop charts. In what was an unusual move for a country act, the album's second chart-topping single, "Teardrops On My Guitar," was released in two separate versions. One was a smooth mix for country radio, while the second featured a stronger beat and vocal arrangement meant for pop audiences. Three more singles from *Taylor Swift* sold more than a million copies each. In 2007 she was so popular that she was booked to open concerts for several top country artists, including Rascal Flatts, Brad Paisley, and George Strait.

When Swift released her second album, *Fearless*, in November 2008, it had the largest opening for any female artist in any musical category that year. Five singles from *Fearless* entered the top ten on both the country and pop charts. Swift's winning streak continued in 2009 as she won numerous awards, including Best Female Video from MTV and Album of the Year from ACM. Swift was also the youngest artist to ever win the CMA's highest honor, the award for Entertainer of the Year. She was one of only six women to win that honor.

Swift's astounding accomplishments continued when her third studio album, *Speak Now,* sold more than a million

Taylor Swift's Keen Observations

Tanya Tucker was a female teenage country music star in the 1970s, and LeAnn Rimes attained that status in the 1990s. Taylor Swift stood apart from earlier teen country sensations, though, because she wrote or cowrote every song on her eponymous debut album. Swift even wrote some of the songs, such as "The Outside," when she was only twelve years old, before she ever even had a boyfriend. Swift commented on her writing inspiration in a December 2006 CMT interview:

You listen to my album and it sounds like I've had 500 boyfriends. But that's really not the case. I found that you don't have to date someone to write a song about them. [When I wrote "The Outside"] I was going through a really tough time in school and facing a lot of rejection among my peers. . . . They really didn't talk to me. In the process of coming to that realization, I started developing this really keen sense of observation—of how to watch people and see what they did. From that sense, I was able to write songs about relationships when I was 13 but not in relationships.

Quoted in Edward Morris. "When She Thinks 'Tim McGraw,' Taylor Swift Savors Payoff." CMT News (2006). www.cmt.com/news/country-music/1546980 /when-she-thinks-tim-mcgraw-taylor-swift-savors -payoff.jhtml.

copies the week after its October 2010 release. By August 2011, sales totaled more than 5.5 million. Like previous Swift efforts, the album blends acoustic country, soft rock, catchy pop production values, and even an occasional Auto-Tune number, referring to the electronic voice effect widely used by Kanye West and other hip-hop acts. Swift's arrangements often stray from the conventional sounds heard on country radio. But her mature songwriting skills and lyrics obviously appeal to a large segment of the country audience.

The dedication of Swift's young fans was seen in Los Angeles in August 2011. All eighty thousand tickets for a four-night stint of her Fearless Tour at the Staples Center sold out in a record-setting two minutes. By the end of the year, Swift's total sales of concert tickets, CDs, and merchandise reached $120 million.

Carrie Underwood Plays On

In the second half of the 2000s, Taylor Swift would have stood alone in her accomplishments if it were not for Carrie Underwood. Born in Muskogee, Oklahoma, in 1983, Underwood learned to play guitar and piano at a young age, developed an amazing four-octave singing range, and performed at local events throughout her childhood. In 2005 she was a contestant on the *American Idol* TV talent show. Underwood's beauty, charm, and strong, pure vocal style helped make her the first country singer to win the compe-

Carrie Underwood, 2005 American Idol winner, performs at the 2011 Stagecoach Country Music Festival in Indio, California.

tition. Her debut single, "Inside Your Heaven," was released soon after.

Thanks to her national television exposure, Underwood's first album, *Some Hearts*, sold three hundred thousand copies in its first week. The album went on to sell more than 10 million copies, making it 2006's number-one selling album in all musical categories.

Unlike Swift, Underwood did not write any of the fourteen songs on her first album. For the follow-up, *Carnival Ride*, Underwood decided to become more involved in the songwriting process. She collaborated with a group of professional Nashville songwriters and cowrote three songs on the 2007 effort. The album debuted at number one on the pop charts and soon went triple platinum. Underwood's third album, 2009's *Play On*, achieved similar success.

By 2010 Underwood had gathered even more music industry awards than Swift, with ten Academy of Country Music awards and fourteen *Billboard* awards compared to Swift's three and seven, respectively. Underwood also seemed to be favored by fans. According to a *Los Angeles Times* poll, Underwood was regarded as a better singer than Swift by a margin of two to one. Regardless of polls or awards, the competition is a winning situation for listeners. With Underwood and Swift vying to outdo one another, they are producing some of the hottest country pop music of the 2010s.

Old and New

Carrie Underwood and Taylor Swift attracted the most attention at the time, but hundreds of artists, new and old, were bringing joy to country music fans. In 2011 relative newcomers like Jason Aldean competed for CMA awards with established artists like Keith Urban, Brad Paisley, and Kenny Chesney. Meanwhile a new crop of artists, including The Band Perry, Thompson Square, and Eric Church, made their marks on country music history.

The style of down-home music conceived in the forests, hollers, and hills of Appalachia in the nineteenth century was polished to a bright sheen in the digital age. Whether the artist was Taylor Swift, Lady Antebellum, the Dixie Chicks, or The Band Perry, musical sounds from long ago remained vital and important. In the 2010s any listener with a discerning ear could tune in to a country radio station and hear echoes of Hank Williams, Bill Monroe, Loretta Lynn, or Patsy Cline in the latest hit record. Like those revered pioneers, modern country artists continue to sing from the heart, tell a good story, and make the audience kick up their heels and dance.

NOTES

Chapter 1: Country Roots

1. Steven D. Price. *Old as the Hills.* New York: Viking Press, 1975, p. 9.
2. Bill C. Malone. *Don't Get Above Your Raisin'.* Urbana: University of Illinois Press, 2002, p. 1.
3. Price. *Old as the Hills,* p. 9.
4. Quoted in Robert K. Oermann. *America's Music: The Roots of Country.* Atlanta: Turner Publishing, 1996, pp. 12–13.
5. Quoted in Robert K. Oermann. *A Century of Country.* New York: TV Books, 1999, p. 11.
6. Quoted in Chet Flippo. "Maybelle Carter." *Rolling Stone* (2011), http://archive.rollingstone.com/ Desktop#/19781214/46.
7. Quoted in Oermann. *America's Music,* p. 37.
8. Quoted in Roy Acuff and William Neely. *Roy Acuff's Nashville.* New York: Perigree Books, 1983, pp. 78–79.
9. Quoted in Oermann. *America's Music,* p. 40.
10. Quoted in Jeffrey J. Lange. *Smile When You Call Me a Hillbilly.* Athens: University of Georgia Press, 2004, p. 59.
11. Quoted in Tom Ewing, ed. *The Bill Monroe Reader.* Chicago: University of Illinois Press, 2000, p. 11.
12. Quoted in Ewing. *Bill Monroe Reader,* p. 31.
13. Quoted in "Tributes." *Rolling Stone* (2011). http://archive.rollingstone .com/Desktop#/19961226/94.
14. Quoted in Oermann. *A Century of Country,* p. 80.
15. Bob Artis. *Bluegrass.* New York: Hawthorn Books, 1975, p. 25.
16. Quoted in Ewing. *Bill Monroe Reader,* p. 179.

Chapter 2: Cowboy Music and Western Swing

17. Malone. *Don't Get Above Your Raisin',* p. 130.
18. Bill C. Malone. *Country Music, U.S.A.* Austin: University of Texas Press, 2002, p. 143.
19. Malone. *Country Music,* p. 143.
20. Quoted in Cary Ginell and Roy Lee Brown. *Milton Brown and the Founding of Western Swing.* Urbana: University of Illinois Press, 1994, p. 63.
21. Quoted in Ginell and Brown. *Milton Brown and the Founding of Western Swing,* p. 109.

22. Kurt Wolff. *Country Music: The Rough Guide*. London: Rough Guides, 2000, p. 94.
23. Wolff. *Country Music*, p. 76.
24. Quoted in Charles R. Townsend. *San Antonio Rose: The Life and Music of Bob Wills*. Urbana: University of Illinois Press, 1976, pp. 268–269.

Chapter 3: Honky-Tonk Music

25. Quoted in Lange. *Smile*, p. 163.
26. Quoted in Nick Tosches. *Country: The Twisted Roots of Rock 'n' Roll*. Cambridge, MA: De Capo Press, p. 27.
27. Quoted in Country Music Foundation. *Country: The Music and Musicians*. New York: Abbeville Press, 1994, p. 161.
28. Quoted in Malone. *Country Music*, p. 193.
29. Wolff. *Country Music*, pp. 158–159.
30. Quoted in Country Music Foundation. *Country*, p. 172.
31. Wolff. *Country Music*, p. 157.
32. Quoted in Nicholas Dawidoff. *In the Country of Country*. New York: Pantheon Books, 1997, p. 64.
33. Quoted in Dawidoff. *In the Country*, p. 64.
34. Quoted in Country Music Foundation. *Country*, p. 226.

Chapter 4: The Nashville Sound

35. Quoted in Diane Pecknold. *The Selling Sound*. Durham: Duke University Press, 2007, p. 90.
36. Quoted in Oermann. *A Century of Country*, p. 154.
37. Quoted in Joli Jensen. *Nashville Sound: Authenticity, Commercialization, and Country Music*. Nashville: Vanderbilt University, 1998, p. 77.
38. Wolff. *Country Music*, p. 315.

Chapter 5: Country Rock and Outlaws

39. Quoted in Peter Doggett. *Are You Ready For the Country*. New York: Penguin Books, 2001, p. 6.
40. Quoted in Clinton Heylin. *Revolution In the Air: The Songs of Bob Dylan 1957–1973*. Chicago: Chicago Review Press, 2009, p. 206.
41. Bob Dylan. *Chronicles*. New York: Simon & Schuster, 2004, p. 95.
42. Barry Gifford. "September 14, 1968." Rolling Stone All Access (2011), http://archive.rollingstone.com/Desktop#/19680914/20.
43. Keith Richards. *Life*. New York: Little, Brown and Company, 2010, p. 73.
44. Quoted in Doggett. *Are You Ready*, p. 156.
45. Quoted in Doggett. *Are You Ready*, p. 63.
46. Richards. *Life*, p. 73.
47. Quoted in Doggett. *Are You Ready*, p. 347.
48. Quoted in "The Bio." Commander Cody (2010), www.commandercody.com.
49. Quoted in "The Bio," Commander

Cody (2010), www.commander
cody.com.

50. Quoted in Doggett. *Are You Ready*,
p. 118.
51. Quoted in Doggett. *Are You Ready*,
p. 119.

Chapter 6: Old and New Traditions

52. Quoted in Wolff. *Country Music*,
p. 424.
53. Wolff. *Country Music*, p. 428.
54. David Dicaire. *The New Generation of Country Music Stars*. Jefferson, NC: McFarland & Company,
2008, p. 7.
55. Wolff. *Country Music*, p. 502.
56. Stephen Thomas Erlewine. "Shania Twain." AllMusic (2011),
www.allmusic.com/artist/shania
-twain-p42121/biography.
57. Quoted in "Shut Up and Sing."
Democracy Now (2007), www
.democracynow.org/2007/2/15
/shut_up_and_sing_dixie_chicks.

Chapter 7: Alt, Progressive, and Pop Country

58. David Dicaire. *The New Generation*, p. 223.
59. Mikael Wood. "Lucinda Williams: Little Honey." *Spin* (2011),
www.spin.com/reviews/lucinda
-williams-little-honey-lost
-highway.
60. Steve Huey. "Car Wheels on a Gravel
Road." AllMusic (2011), www.all
music.com/album/car-wheels-on
-a-gravel-road-r352237/review.
61. Stephen Thomas Erlewine.
"Shock'n Y'All." AllMusic (2011),
www.allmusic.com/album
/shockn-yall-r666010/review.
62. Quoted in "Toby Keith's USO Tour
Underway." CMT News (2011),
www.cmt.com/news/news-in
-brief/1662677/toby-keiths-uso
-tour-underway.jhtml.

Garth Brooks

No Fences, 1990

Ropin' the Wind, 1991

Brooks & Dunn

Brand New Man, 1991

With three smash singles including the line dancing hit "Boot Scoot Boogie," this album introduced a new country sound that catapulted the duo of Kix Brooks and Ronnie Dunn to the top of the country charts, where they remained for nearly two decades.

Milton Brown

Essential Western Swing, 2003

The Byrds

Sweetheart of the Rodeo, 1968

Recorded with Gram Parsons, this was the first country record by any major rock group. The old-time, religious-themed songs such as "I Am a Pilgrim" and "Christian Life" alienated a large segment of the Byrds' audience, and the record failed to crack the top-fifty album charts. Today the record is recognized as a landmark country rock album that influenced the outlaw country and new traditionalist movements.

The Carter Family

RCA Country Legends: The Carter Family, 2004

Neko Case

Fox Confessor Brings the Flood, 2007

Middle Cyclone, 2009

Kenny Chesney

Super Hits, 2007

Hemingway's Whiskey, 2010

Kenny Chesney's fourteenth studio album produced three number-one hits celebrating new country music, partying, and island beats.

The Dixie Chicks

Wide Open Spaces, 1998

With three top-ten hits, this album helped make the Dixie Chicks the hottest act in country and by 2006, the album was the best-selling group album in country music history. The sound is pure Dixie Chicks, with hot picking, gorgeous singing, tight country harmonies, and two-step dance beats.

Bob Dylan

Nashville Skyline, 1969

This album kicks off with a duet with Johnny Cash and continues with peppy guitar, fiddle, and pedal steel tunes that showcase Bob Dylan's new countrified crooning voice. Fans were shocked by the short, simple country songs that celebrated rural values during a turbulent decade, but the single "Lay, Lady, Lay" remains Dylan's biggest pop hit.

The Eagles

Their Greatest Hits (1971–1975), 1976

This compilation showcases the cool California country rock sounds that inspired generations of musicians and songwriters.

The Flying Burrito Brothers

The Definitive Collection, 2002

Although the Flying Burrito Brothers carried on after Gram Parsons quit in 1970, most country rock fans agree the band was never the same. This compilation includes the two complete albums the Burritos made while Parsons was still a member of the group he founded.

The Judds

Number One Hits, 1994

These songs made the mother-daughter duo one of the most successful acts in country music history. Traditional Appalachian harmonies and bluegrass and honky-tonk elements give these hits a timeless quality that sounds fresh decades after they were recorded.

Toby Keith

Unleashed, 2002

Keith's second platinum album soared to the top of the country charts driven by his unabashed outlaw outlook, perhaps best expressed in "Courtesy of the Red, White and Blue (The Angry American)." In addition to his political viewpoint, Keith's hard-drinking, honky tonk anthems made Unleashed a welcome antidote to the pop country that was dominating radio at the time.

Clancy's Tavern, 2011

Lady Antebellum

Need You Now, 2010

k.d. lang

Shadowland, 1988

This albums is k.d. lang's tribute to 1940s and 1950s honky-tonk. While there is an campy element to the project, the rich, soaring vocals give the listener shivers up the spine as lang does her best to sound like a reincarnation of country icon Patsy Cline.

Absolute Torch and Twang, 1989

Reba McEntire

My Kind of Country, 1984

Whoever's in New England, 1986

Reba McEntire embraced new traditionalism in the mid-1980s and started writing country songs from a feminist perspective that spoke to women of her generation. This album began a run of top-ten McEntire albums that lasted nearly a decade.

Keep on Loving You, 2009

Bill Monroe & His Bluegrass Boys

Bill Monroe: Anthology, 2003

This collection features fifty hits recorded over the course of two decades by the founding father of bluegrass music. It covers classics such as "Uncle Pen," "Blue Moon of Kentucky," and "Mule Skinner Blues."

The Nitty Gritty Dirt Band

Will the Circle Be Unbroken, 1972

This album kicked off the 1970s bluegrass revival, introducing Maybelle Carter, Jimmy Martin, Roy Acuff, Merle Travis, Earl Scruggs, Doc Watson, and other bluegrass pioneers to rock and pop music fans.

Buck Owens

21 #1 Hits: The Ultimate Collection, 2006

Dolly Parton

16 Biggest Hits, 2007

This anthology contains the best of the best from Parton's most productive period in the 1970s and 1980s, including the classics "Joleen" and "9 to 5."

Dolly Parton and Porter Wagoner

Duets, 1967

This album features the famed duet that racked up dozens of number-one hits in the late '60s and early '70s. The smooth arrangements are pure countrypolitan, and Parton's standout vocals helped launch her solo career.

Rascal Flatts

Unstoppable, 2006

Tight harmonies, hot-guitar licks, and high lonesome pedal steel guitars drive the aching pop country love songs that made this trio one of the best-selling country bands of the 2000s.

Elvis Presley, Jerry Lee Lewis, Carl Perkins, and Johnny Cash

The Complete Million Dollar Quartet, 2006

In December 1956, the biggest rock stars in the world, all raised on country music, got together for an impromptu jam session as the tapes were rolling at Sun Records in Memphis, Tennessee.

Jim Reeves

The Essential Jim Reeves, 2005

This comprehensive compilation features forty of Reeves's top hits recorded before his untimely death. Songs range from the corny and silly "Beatin' on the Ding Dong" to countrypolitan crooner classics like "He'll Have to Go."

LeAnn Rimes

Blue, 1996

LeAnn Rimes was only thirteen years old when she recorded her debut album, but her age belied a grown-up voice that could hold its own against country giants such as Patsy, Loretta, or Dolly. This album still stands out even in an era of country rap and bluegrass pop.

This Woman, 2005

Jimmie Rodgers

The Very Best Of, 2009

The Very Best Of showcases the greatest hits by the Singing Brakeman, who put hillbilly music at the top of the pop charts before his untimely death in 1933.

George Strait

50 Number One Hits, 2004

Two full CDs were required to capture the astounding number of chart-topping singles produced by the most successful neotraditionalist in country music. The tunes evoke Lefty Frizzell, Hank Williams, and Merle Haggard, while showing off Strait's trademark brand of earnestness, honesty, and elegance.

Taylor Swift

Taylor Swift, 2006

Fearless, 2008

Taylor Swift's second album produced five top-ten singles, broke several country music sales records, and made the nineteen-year-old singer, with her unique brand of country pop music, an international star.

Merle Travis

In Boston, 1959, 2003

Shania Twain

The Woman in Me, 1995

Come On Over, 1997

Carrie Underwood

Some Hearts, 2006

Play On, 2009

Hank Williams

20th Century Masters—The Millennium Collection: The Best of Hank Williams, Vol 2, 2006

This collection is a great introduction to the man who lived the honky-tonk blues and includes Hank Williams's greatest hits "Hey, Good Lookin'," "Jambalaya," "I Saw the Light," and "Lovesick Blues."

Lucinda Williams

Sweet Old World, 1992

Car Wheels on a Gravel Road, 1998

On her breakout alt-country album, Lucinda Williams takes the listener on a tour of the Deep South, spinning brilliant musical melodramas whose catchy choruses and memorable melodies belie the themes of longing, heartbreak, murder, suicide, and abuse.

Little Honey, 2008

Bob Wills & His Texas Playboys

For the Last Time, 1994

Although Texas swing pioneer Bob Wills died during the last days of recording, he was able to watch his talented band get together one last time to record classics such as "Rose of San Antone" and "Faded Love" that changed the sound of country music, inflecting it with jazz, boogie-woogie, and blues.

Various Artists

Cowboy Songs, 2010

This iTunes compilation features Gene Autry, Roy Rogers, the Sons of the Pioneers, Patsy Montana, and Tex Ritter, as well as more-modern cowboys like the Eagles and Randy Travis.

Grand Ole Opry Broadcasts, Volumes 1, 2, and 3, 2010

These compilations take the listener back to a time when Hank Williams, Roy Acuff, Tex Ritter, the Carter Family, and dozens of other country pioneers could be heard on the radio playing live every Saturday night.

O Brother, Where Art Thou?, 2000

Urban Cowboy: Original Motion Picture Soundtrack, 1995

Wanted! The Outlaws, 1996

Originally released in 1976, this influential collaboration between Waylon Jennings, Willie Nelson, Tompall Glaser, and Jessi Colter was the biggest-selling country album in history at the time and defined the country outlaw sound that influenced musicians for generations.

Will the Circle Be Unbroken, 1972

album: Originally used to describe a twelve-inch (30cm) vinyl, long-playing (LP) record that played at 33 rpm (revolutions per minute) and could hold about twenty minutes of music on each side. In the digital age, an album is any collection of songs released together by a single artist.

artists and repertoire: Known as A&R, this is a system in which a music industry professional chooses songs for an artist to perform, hires musicians for recording, and oversees artistic development.

ballad: A song, usually in a slow tempo, that tells a story.

counterculture: During the 1960s millions of young Americans were called hippies or members of the counterculture when they took drugs such as marijuana and LSD, dressed in bright colors, grew long hair, and protested war and corporate power.

Dobro: A type of guitar with a large metal resonator attached to the face of the instrument that is played with a slide bar.

gold: A term used for records that sell more than five hundred thousand copies.

neotraditional: A style of music pioneered by George Strait in the late 1980s that blends "back-to-basics" traditional country styles such as honky-tonk and swing with modern genres including rock and blues.

pedal steel guitar: A type of horizontal electric guitar on which players use a metal bar, foot pedals, and knee levers to change the pitch of the notes. With its sliding chords, bending notes, and quick picked riffs, the pedal steel is one of the most distinctive instruments in country music.

platinum: A term used to describe records that sell more than 1 million copies. Multiplatinum records sell more than 2 million copies.

producer: In music, a producer works with a band to manage and oversee the recording process.

single: Originally any record with a single song on each side. In the 1950s singles were sold as seven-inch (17.7cm) vinyl records that played at 45 rpm. In the digital age, a single is any one song that is promoted separately from an album.

FOR MORE INFORMATION

Books

Bob Allen and Tony Byworth. *The Billboard Illustrated Encyclopedia of Country Music*. New York: Billboard Books, 2007. This book explores country music with short biographies and hundreds of photos, following the style's development through the twentieth century up to recent years. Chapters trace the history of early hillbilly music, bluegrass, honky-tonk, rockabilly, country rock, outlaws, neotraditionalists, and more.

Richard Carlin. *American Popular Music: Country*. New York: Facts on File, 2012. This title covers American country music traditions from the balladry of the British Isles to western swing, honky-tonk, and the modern sounds of the twenty-first century.

Cherese Cartlidge. *Taylor Swift*. Farmington Hills, MI: Lucent Books, 2012. This book reveals how Taylor Swift's unusual poise and talent in crafting memorable, often poetic lines has helped propel her into a music star. Swift's inspirations, romantic life, home life, charitable work, and hobbies are also discussed.

David Dicaire. *The New Generation of Country Music Stars*. Jefferson, NC: McFarland & Company, 2008. *The New Generation* contains short biographies of fifty country music stars born after 1940, and is divided into chapters such as New Traditionalists, Alternative Country, Groups, Country Pop, and Contemporary Country.

Editors of People magazine. *PEOPLE Country's Biggest Stars!: And the Stories Behind Their Best-Known Songs*. New York: People, 2011. This book features the biggest names in country music today, showcasing their lives in photos and interviews, the towns they grew up in, early career successes, and how they live today.

Vernell Hackett. *Carrie Underwood: A Biography*. Santa Barbara: Greenwood, 2010. This biography follows the singer's career arc from a small town in Oklahoma to *American Idol* and the most prestigious concert halls in the world.

Wilborn Hampton. *Elvis Presley*. London: Puffin, 2008. This entry records events in Elvis Presley's ascent to fame, describing his impact on rock and roll, country music, and the music industry in general.

Brett Mitchells. *The Dixie Chicks*. New York: Rosen Publishing Group, 2008. This story of one of the most popular, and controversial, country acts of the 2000s contains biographical information about the group's members, how the band found success, and how it continued on after lead singer Natalie Maines's 2003 criticism of President George W. Bush.

Tony Russell. *Country Music Originals: The Legends and the Lost*. New York: Oxford University Press, 2010. Graced by more than two hundred photos, many of them seldom seen and some never before published, this volume offers vivid portraits of the men and women who created country music, including Jimmie Rodgers, the Carter Family, Fiddlin' John Carson, and Gene Autry.

Andrew Vaughan. *Taylor Swift*. New York: Sterling, 2011. This book celebrates the country pop singer with a wealth of photographs, album artwork, and archive memorabilia while tracing Swift's achievements, music, and philanthropy.

Edward Willett. *Johnny Cash: The Man in Black*. Berkeley Heights, NJ: Enslow Publishers, 2010. This biography follows the life and career of America's most famous country singer, focusing on his rebellious side and beginning with his famous 1968 live-album recording at California's Folsom State Prison.

Sara McIntosh Wooten. *Tim McGraw: Celebrity with Heart*. Berkeley Heights, NJ: Enslow Publishers, 2010. This books describes Tim McGraw's tough childhood, his long, hard road to success, his musical triumphs, and his relationship with his wife and growing family.

Internet

Academy of Country Music (ACM) (www.acmcountry.com). Based in California, ACM was founded in 1964 to promote country music in the western states, mainly the Bakersfield sound pioneered by Buck Owens, Merle Haggard, and others. The group's website is largely dedicated to the prestigious ACM Awards show and includes photos, videos, news, and information about the biggest country stars of the day.

AllMusic (www.allmusic.com/explore/genre/country-d27). First known as All Music Guide (AMG), the AllMusic website is one of the most comprehensive music guides on the Internet. The Country, Alternative Country-Rock, and Americana sections contain hundreds of album reviews and artist biographies. The site also has sections on a wide variety of country sounds, including progressive country, honky-tonk, folk country, and western swing.

Brad's Page of Steel (www.well.com/user/wellvis/steel.html). This is one of the most comprehensive sites on the Web dedicated to the steel guitar. Different types of steel guitars are defined, including lap, pedal steel, Hawaiian style, and slide. Links to manufacturers, tunings, and playing lessons are provided. The site also includes biographies of steel guitar greats such as Leon McAuliffe, Bob Dunn, Junior Brown, and Buddy Emmons.

CMT (www.cmt.com). The home of Country Music Television, this website features country music news, artist biographies, thousands of music videos, and replays of the channel's popular TV shows.

Country Music Association (CMA) (www.cmaworld.com). The CMA was founded in 1958 as a trade organization to promote country music throughout the world. Their website features wide coverage of country music news, events, awards shows, festivals, and artist biographies.

No Depression (www.nodepression .com). No Depression has been covering Americana, alt-country, and roots music since 1995. The site has archives, photos, blogs, videos, festival listings, and music news.

Roughstock (www.roughstock.com). Roughstock has been providing the latest in country music news, album reviews, lyrics, songs, and music videos since 1993 and covers a variety of styles, including bluegrass, Americana, alt-country, and mainstream country music.

Films

Coal Miner's Daughter, 1980
Sissy Spacek won a Grammy for her portrayal of Loretta Lynn in this biopic about the poor Kentucky mountain girl who rose to stardom and became the "Queen of Country Music."

O Brother, Where Art Thou?, 2000
This comedy, starring George Clooney, John Goodman, and Holly Hunter, is set in rural Mississippi in 1937 and follows three men who escape from a chain gang. As part of the plot, the main characters pose as a old-time string band called the Soggy Bottom Boys. The movie's soundtrack album, featuring Alison Krauss, Emmylou Harris, Gillian Welch, John Hartford, and other prominent country stars, sold more than 8 million copies and renewed popular interest in bluegrass music.

The Johnny Cash Show: The Best of Johnny Cash 1969–1971, 2007
Johnny Cash graced America's TV airwaves for only a brief period, but during his show's short run the roster of legendary musical guests included Waylon Jennings, Marty Robbins, Tammy Wynette, Bill Monroe & His Bluegrass Boys, Merle Haggard, Joni Mitchell, and Bob Dylan. Their performances, captured on this DVD, are priceless.

Urban Cowboy, 1980
John Travolta is a dancing, bull riding, heartbreaking urban cowboy in this legendary film, which touched off the urban cowboy fad, inspiring millions of urban and suburban viewers alike to don boots, jeans, and cowboy hats and dance to country music.

Walk the Line, 2005

Joaquin Phoenix and Reese Witherspoon take viewers on a musical journey as they depict the lives of country music legends Johnny Cash and June Carter Cash.

INDEX

PICTURE CREDITS

Cover image: Len Green/Shutterstock
.com

© Anwar Hussein/Hulton Archive/
Getty Images, 75

AP Images/Dan Poush, 76

AP Images/Michael Tweed, 81

© Chris Hellier/Corbis, 14

© David Atlas/Retna Ltd./Corbis, 111

© David Redfern/Redferns/Getty Images, 98

© Eric Schaal/Time Life Pictures/
Getty Images, 18

© Frank Driggs Collection/Getty Images, 24, 43

© Frank Driggs/Michael Ochs Ar-
chives/Getty Images, 38

© Gems/Redferns/Getty Images, 27

© Jim McCrary/Redferns/Getty Images, 79

© Kevin Winter/Getty Images, 114

© Michael Ochs Archives/Getty Images, 21, 33, 41, 50, 52, 57, 64, 68

© Paul Natkin/WireImage/Getty Images, 93, 100

© RCA Records/Frank Driggs Collec-
tion/Getty Images, 90

© Rick Friedman/Corbis, 95

© Robin Platzer/Time & Life Pictures/
Getty Images, 66

© Samantha Shrader/Retna Ltd./Cor-
bis, 10

© Silver Screen Collection/Hulton
Archive/Getty Images, 69, 87

© Tim Mosenfelder/Corbis, 104, 108

© Yale Joel/Time & Life Pictures/Getty
Images, 48

ABOUT THE AUTHOR

Stuart A. Kallen is the author of more than 250 nonfiction books for children and young adults. He has written extensively about science, the environment, music, culture, history, and folklore. In addition, Mr. Kallen has written award-winning children's videos and television scripts. In his spare time, he is a singer/songwriter/guitarist in San Diego, California.